A QUICK COURSE IN

DOS

Version 5

JOYCE COX

KJELL SWEDIN

PUBLISHED BY
Online Press Incorporated
14320 NE 21st Street, Suite 18
Bellevue, WA 98007
(206) 641-3434

Publisher's Cataloging in Publication
(prepared by Quality Books Inc.)

Cox, Joyce, 1946–
   A Quick Course in DOS, version 5 / Joyce Cox, Kjell Swedin. —
  p. cm.
  Includes index.
  ISBN 1-879399-03-2

  1. DOS 5.0 (Computer operating system). 2. Operating systems
(Computers) I. Swedin, Kjell, 1958– II. Title.

QA76.76.O63   005.4'46
                                  QBI91-168
                                        91-60421
                                        CIP

Printed and bound in the United States of America

1 2 3 4 5 6 7 8 9 G L O L 3 2 1 0

Distributed to bookstores by Publishers Group West, (800) 365-3453

UNIX® is a registered trademark of American Telephone and Telegraph Company. Apple® and Macintosh® are registered trademarks of Apple Computing, Inc. Quattro® and Quattro Pro® are registered trademarks of Borland International, Inc. PC Tools Deluxe™ is a trademark of Central Point Software, Inc. IBM® is a registered trademark of International Business Machines Corporation. 386™ is a trademark of Intel Corporation. Lotus® and 1-2-3® are registered trademarks of Lotus Development Corporation. Windows™ is a trademark and Microsoft® is a registered trademark of Microsoft Corporation. WordPerfect® is a registered trademark of WordPerfect Corporation. All other products mentioned in this book are trademarks of their respective owners.

Contents

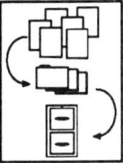

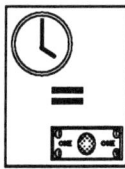
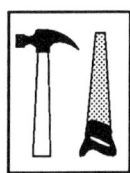

Introduction

For months, people have been asking us "When will your DOS book be available?" Why are people so interested in a *new* book about DOS? Because DOS is not an easy program for most new users to understand—it takes time. And because it helps to have a basic understanding of the workings of DOS to do useful work with your computer.

So what are people looking for in a book about DOS? Here's what we found out.

First, people are looking for a book they can digest quickly. (They would much rather be reading the latest best-seller or playing with the kids than putting in time with a computer book.) That's why they're looking to us. *Quick Course* books have a reputation for cutting through the clutter and delivering clear, concise instructions for using today's most popular software programs.

Second, most people want to be able to sit back after performing a specific task, having gained an understanding of exactly what they did and why—knowing that next time, they'll be able to perform a similar task with a lot less effort. *Quick Course* books don't simply tell you *how* to perform a task; they explain *what* you're doing and *why* you're doing it.

Third, some people are looking for a quick, no-nonsense way to learn about DOS 5's new features so that they can easily incorporate them into an existing repertoire of DOS procedures. For these DOS veterans, we offer a fast way to come up to speed with the latest DOS version.

Like other books in the *Quick Course* series, *A Quick Course in DOS* doesn't cover every last product feature. We focus on those features you need to know to make DOS a useful part of your work environment. We show you how to give commands from both the Shell and the command line so that you can choose which approach works best for you; we suggest ways of organizing your files and setting up procedures to enhance your efficiency; we talk about the DOS features that help you recover from mistakes and maintain your system; and we look at ways to get your work done more efficiently. In addition to all this, we include a time-saving table that lets you quickly look up the command you need in order to perform the task at hand. We end our discussion of DOS with an alphabetical reference that includes most of the commands that come with DOS, offering brief scenarios to help you see why and how you might use each command.

Along the way, we offer handy tips and useful tidbits. When you have the time, you can look them over and learn even more about DOS. And, for those times when you need to refer back to a particular discussion or want to browse ahead, we use arrows and captions to draw your attention to various procedures, commands, or functions so that you can easily spot them later on as you thumb through the book.

As we have said, learning DOS is by no means an easy task, but you don't have to tackle it all at once. Each chapter in *A Quick Course in DOS* focuses on a different topic, progressing from everyday chores to more advanced procedures. Take a moment to quickly flip through the book and see what we have in store for you. Then turn to Chapter 1, and let's get started.

1

First Things First

Y ou don't need to learn more than a few DOS basics to use your computer. But knowing a bit about DOS can make you more efficient and productive. And if anything goes wrong with your files, your disks, or your system, understanding DOS will save you some anguish and may save you time and money. In this book, our goal is to cover just enough for you to be able to take full advantage of the many tools DOS provides.

What Is DOS?

DOS stands for *disk operating system*. This term is somewhat misleading, because DOS actually controls a lot more than just your disks. It coordinates all your computer's *hardware*—the central processing unit (CPU), hard drive, floppy drive(s), monitor, keyboard, mouse, and other devices—by means of *software*—computer programs. When you work on your computer, you work with two kinds of software: system programs (like DOS) and application programs. Let's discuss application programs first.

Two kinds of software

Application programs allow you to perform specific types of tasks. For example, you can construct spreadsheet models with spreadsheet application programs such as Microsoft Excel, and you can write reports with word-processing application programs such as WordPerfect. On the surface, a spreadsheet program and a word-processing program might seem very different, but many functions are common to both programs. For example, they need to respond to keyboard instructions, retrieve files from a hard disk or floppy disk, change information in the files, show information on the screen, and save it on disk. Each application program could provide its own instructions for these routine tasks, but long ago software developers realized it would be more efficient to have one set of programs carry out these basic chores for all application programs.

System programs were developed to fill this need, and collections of system programs designed to work together became known as an *operating system*. By managing files and hardware devices (such as your monitor, keyboard, and disk drives) and overseeing basic system operations, an operating system provides a foundation for the application programs that are designed to work with, or *run under*, it. Common operating systems are DOS, UNIX, and Apple OS. You may also have heard of CP/M (which was popular in the 1970s), DR DOS, Xenix, and OS/2.

Why don't we include Microsoft Windows as an example of an operating system? Because Windows is an *environment*, not an operating system. In fact, Windows works with DOS, just like application programs for PCs and compatibles do. You cannot use Windows unless you have DOS.

Historically, several operating systems have battled for supremacy in the lucrative personal-computer marketplace, but since the early 1980s, the primary operating system for IBM personal computers and compatible machines has been DOS, the name commonly used to refer to Microsoft's operating system. (You might also see DOS referred to as MS-DOS or PC-DOS.)

The Anatomy of DOS

You don't need to know details about the components of DOS to use it. But for those of you who are interested, we'll pause for a moment to give you some background information about the programs that make up the DOS operating system. Feel free to skip this section if you're anxious to move on.

What exactly is DOS? When you install DOS on your computer, the following program files are copied to the hard disk: two hidden files (MSDOS.SYS and IO.SYS), a command processor (COMMAND.COM), and a collection of other operating-system programs.

Background information

Generally, you will never have to deal with the two hidden files. MSDOS.SYS contains the heart of DOS, known as the *DOS kernel*. IO.SYS is a system initialization program that gets DOS running when you turn on, or *boot*, your computer. Because these files are so important to DOS, they are hidden from you (meaning that their names are not displayed when you request a list of the files in your root directory, which we discuss in a minute). Hiding the files prevents you from inadvertently doing anything with them, such as deleting them or moving them so that DOS can't find them. For DOS to work, they need to stay exactly where the installation program puts them.

The command processor, called COMMAND.COM, is the part of DOS that helps you carry out common tasks, such as copying and moving files, deleting files, and creating directories. (We explain these commands in detail in Chapter 3.) COMMAND.COM is made up of a number of commands known as *internal commands*. Typing an internal command and pressing Enter carries out the command. For example, typing *ver* (for *version*) and pressing Enter displays the DOS version number; typing *dir* (for *directory*) and pressing Enter displays a list of the files in your root directory (described on page 7).

Finally, commands for carrying out less common tasks, such as comparing files and formatting disks, are processed by the separate system programs that are part of DOS. When you install DOS, these system programs are put in a subdirectory of the root directory. (Unless you specify otherwise during the installation process, this subdirectory is called DOS.) That way, the programs are available for use at any time, but they don't clutter up your root directory.

Terms You May Need to Know

Like any industry, the computer industry has its own jargon. Before we move on, let's go over a few terms that might come up as you learn more about your computer and DOS. You might have heard some of the following terms, but others might be new to you.

8086, 8088, 80286, 80386, and 80486

These terms refer to computer types—specifically to the chip around which a computer is built. These chips are manufactured by Intel. Usually, the five-digit numbers are shortened to 286, 386, and 486. The higher the number, the faster, more powerful, and generally more expensive the computer.

Byte, Kilobyte, and Megabyte

These terms are used to indicate size—the amount of space needed to store a file, the amount of free space available in your computer's memory, and so on. A byte is the smallest unit you are likely to run into. It is the amount of space necessary to store one character—the letter *P* for example. A kilobyte is approximately one thousand bytes (1024 to be exact) and is often abbreviated *KB* or just *K*. A megabyte is approximately one million bytes (1,048,576), and you see it abbreviated as *MB*. For comparison, one double-spaced, 8-1/2-by-11-inch page of text holds about 1,500 characters—that's 1,500 bytes, or 1.5 KB, of information.

Memory

Computers have several types of memory, and not surprisingly, people get confused about which type is which. Let's try to set things straight.

ROM   This term means read-only memory. ROM contains a set of instructions permanently encoded on special ROM chips in your computer. It is stable memory, meaning that it cannot be erased or altered. Because it is permanent, you usually don't have to worry about it.

Read-only memory

RAM   This term means random-access memory. Information in RAM is not stable, meaning that you can make changes to information in RAM and, unless you save the information on disk, it is lost when you turn off your computer. Like ROM, RAM comes in the form of chips inside the computer. Nowadays, computers generally come with 640 KB of RAM (often referred to as *conventional memory*). In addition to conventional memory, many computers also have extended or expanded memory.

Random-access memory

Conventional memory

Extended and expanded memory   Extended and expanded memory are two different forms of add-in RAM. By add-in, we mean that you add it to the base amount of conventional memory. You might need the extra memory to run large application programs, or to enable your machine to run more efficiently. For most people, understanding the difference between extended and expanded memory is not important. However, knowing whether your machine has extended or expanded memory is handy—for example, when you are trying to figure out whether you have enough memory to run a large application program. Fortunately, finding out how

Add-in memory

much memory your computer has is not hard. Assuming that you have already installed DOS 5 on your machine, you might want to try this:

1. If you see the words *MS-DOS Shell* in the title bar at the top of your screen, hold down the Shift key and press F9. Your screen clears, and you see the command prompt (C:\> or C>). If the command prompt is already on your screen, skip this step.

2. Type *mem* (for *memory*), and press Enter. DOS displays a report of your computer's memory, like this:

Getting a memory report

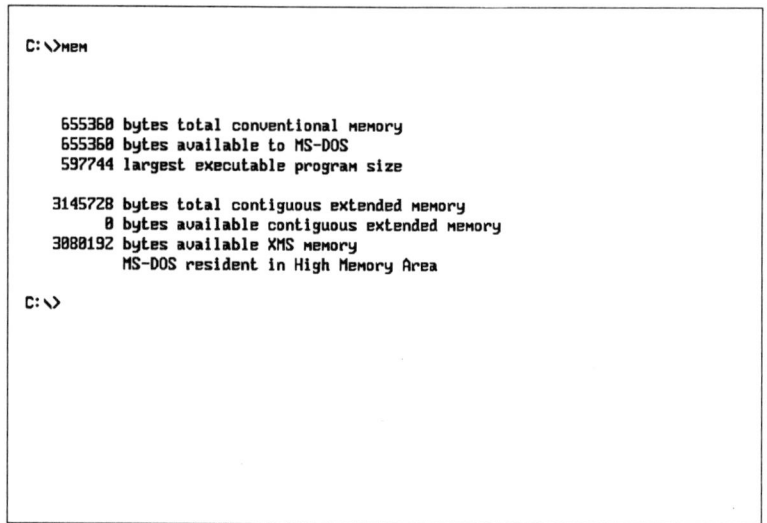

```
C:\>mem


    655360 bytes total conventional memory
    655360 bytes available to MS-DOS
    597744 largest executable program size

   3145728 bytes total contiguous extended memory
         0 bytes available contiguous extended memory
   3080192 bytes available XMS memory
           MS-DOS resident in High Memory Area

C:\>
```

If you have extended or expanded memory, the report for your computer looks much like the one above. DOS tells you that your machine has *EMS memory* if you have expanded memory, or that it has *XMS memory* or *contiguous extended memory* if you have extended memory. If DOS tells you that your machine has both types of memory, you probably have extended memory, some of which is being converted by a memory-management program into expanded memory. If you have neither extended nor expanded memory, you see only the conventional-memory report (the first three lines of the report shown above).

Disk Memory

This term refers to the storage space on your hard disk. When you load a file from your hard disk into a word processor and make changes to it, those changes take place in RAM. When you instruct the word processor to save the file, it transfers the information from RAM to your hard disk where it is stored in disk memory.

Hard-disk storage capacities commonly range from 20 MB to over 100 MB. Some hard disks can store as much as several gigabytes. (One gigabyte—1 GB—is approximately one billion bytes.)   *Hard disks*

Floppy-disk storage capacities commonly range from 360 KB to 1.44 MB, but capacities of up to 2.88 MB are available. Floppy disks come in two sizes: 5.25 inches and 3.5 inches.   *Floppy disks*
The 5.25-inch disks are enclosed in thin protective covers and are truly floppy. The 3.5-inch disks are enclosed in a rigid plastic cover but are nevertheless referred to as floppy disks. Each size of floppy disk is available in two storage capacities: 5.25-inch floppies can store either 360 KB (low density) or 1.2 MB (high density) of information; 3.5-inch floppies can store either 720 KB (low density) or 1.44 MB (high density). These days, most floppy-disk drives can accept both low-density and high-density disks, but some earlier generations of drives can accept only low-density disks.

Monochrome, CGA, EGA, and VGA

These designations all refer to the type of monitor your computer has. Monochrome generally refers to a monitor that can display text only (no graphics) in two colors. CGA, EGA, and VGA refer to monitors that can display text and graphics in two or more colors. They are distinguished by their *resolution*, or clarity, which is determined by the number of *pixels*, or picture elements (a fancy term for dots), that make up the screen.

The Root Directory

When you install DOS on your computer, a root directory, or main directory, is created on your hard drive. All subdirectories (such as the DOS directory discussed on page 4) "branch" from this root directory. (We say "branch" because some people find it helpful to think of their directory structure as a tree.) Some subdirectories have sub-subdirectories branching from them. In the Shell, which we discuss in detail in Chapter 2, the root directory and its subdirectories are represented something like this:

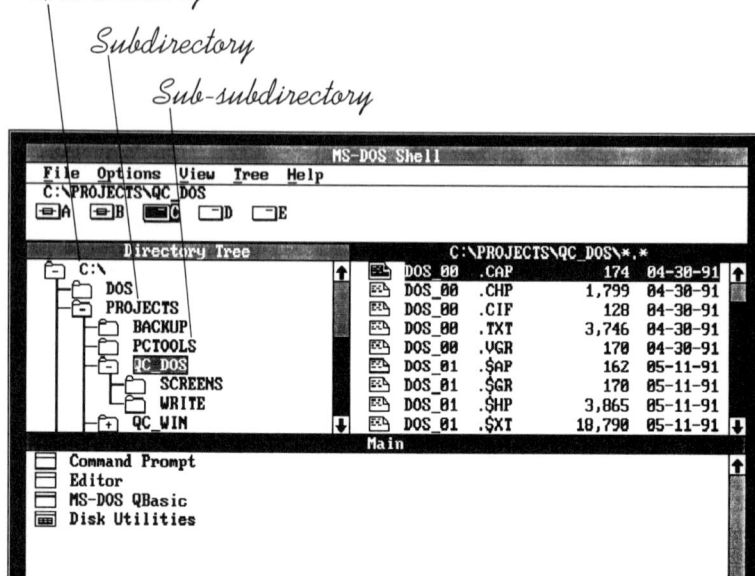

Root directory

Subdirectory

Sub-subdirectory

Directories

Directories are important for a couple of reasons. First, DOS limits the number of files you can store in the root directory, so creating directories is necessary if you want to store a large number of files. Second, and perhaps more important, directories are the key to organizing information on your hard disk. For a complete discussion of directory structure and organization see Chapter 3.

AUTOEXEC.BAT and CONFIG.SYS

The AUTOEXEC.BAT and CONFIG.SYS files are two special files that DOS examines each time you turn on your computer. If you didn't have these files on your system before DOS 5 was installed, the installation program created them for you.

The AUTOEXEC.BAT file is a batch file (see page 86 for information about batch files). Like other batch files, it contains a set of DOS commands, and it has a BAT extension. Unlike other batch files, it is automatically executed (hence the name AUTOEXEC) each time you turn on your machine.

In the next chapter, we will examine the AUTOEXEC.BAT file and learn how to make modifications to it.

The CONFIG.SYS file contains information about how your system should be configured. Unless you are adding software to your system or trying to maximize it's performance (see page 101), you can probably ignore this file.

What's New with DOS 5?

If you're a fairly new computer user, DOS 5 may be the only operating system you have used. Those of you who are switching to DOS 5 from DOS 3 or DOS 4 have some pleasant surprises in store.

To start with, DOS is now easier to install. The new installation program leads you step-by-step through the procedure and provides help at all stages.

Perhaps the most noticeable change with DOS 5 is its graphical interface—the Shell. (The term *graphical interface* is simply a fancy name for the screen and the elements on it that allow you and your computer to communicate.) The DOS 5 Shell is a significant improvement over the shell included with DOS 4. You might think that this improvement would involve a cost in efficiency, but in fact the new Shell takes up less memory and is faster than the DOS 4 shell. It includes a Task Swapper that allows you to switch quickly from one application to another. (For example, you can move from a spreadsheet to a word processor and back again without having to quit or reload either program.) For many people, the Shell may be the single biggest advantage DOS 5 has over previous versions of DOS.

In spite of the Shell's convenience, some people will avoid the graphical interface and will continue to enter commands at the command prompt. If you are part of this crowd, you'll be glad to know that you can now get online information about all DOS commands. If you forget the structure, or *syntax*, of a particular command, you no longer have to look it up in the manual; you simply type the command name followed by /?, and DOS displays the correct syntax, with descriptions of the syntax elements.

The DOS Shell

Task Swapper

Help with commands

Memory management →

File undeleting →

What else is new? If your computer has extended memory, DOS now has the ability to load into your computer's high-memory area instead of taking up conventional memory. As a result, you have more conventional memory available for your programs.

DOS 5 includes several new utility programs, perhaps the most important of which is Undelete, an external command that recovers deleted files. If you have ever experienced the unique feeling of frustration and loss that comes from accidentally deleting a day's work, this addition alone may be sufficient reason for upgrading to DOS 5.

Well, that's it for our quick tour. In the next chapter, we explore the DOS Shell. By making DOS's internal and external commands less cryptic and therefore less intimidating, the Shell may entice you to learn more about DOS and about how it can help you better organize your work and your time.

2

Two DOS Views

DOS only does one thing by itself: It loads itself into memory when you turn on your computer. Thereafter, it does only what you tell it to do. You can give DOS instructions in two ways. You can use the Shell, which enables you to choose commands from lists, called *menus*, or you can type commands at the command prompt, known as *using the command line*. Both methods have advantages and disadvantages.

If you are new to DOS, you'll probably find it easiest to start by using the DOS Shell. With the Shell, you don't have to remember the name and structure of every command you want to use. You simply select the command from a menu, and DOS prompts you for any information it needs to carry out the command. Also displayed in the Shell is a diagram that shows the directories you have created to hold your files, making it easy for you to switch from one directory to another.

As you gain experience with DOS, you may find that you prefer the stripped-down efficiency of the command line. Using the command line is fast and direct, but requires knowledge of the DOS commands and their structure, or *syntax*. Using the command line can be frustrating if you are not an accurate typist, because you must type the commands exactly as DOS expects them.

In this chapter, we take a look at both the Shell and the command line. We'll work with the Shell first.

Visual DOS: The Shell

We assume that you have turned on your computer and that you are ready to go. Some of you may have the DOS Shell on the screen in front of you; others may bc looking at the command prompt (C>). Whether the Shell is automatically displayed when you turn on your computer is a function of a decision made by whoever installed DOS on your machine (see Appendix A) and whether a different shell program, such as Norton Commander or PC Shell (part of PC Tools Deluxe) has been installed on your computer. If you see the words *MS-DOS Shell* at the top of your screen, you are in the Shell and you don't need to do anything. If you don't see these words, start the Shell by typing *dosshell* at the command prompt and pressing Enter. DOS reads the directories and files on your hard disk, and when it finishes, your screen looks something like this:

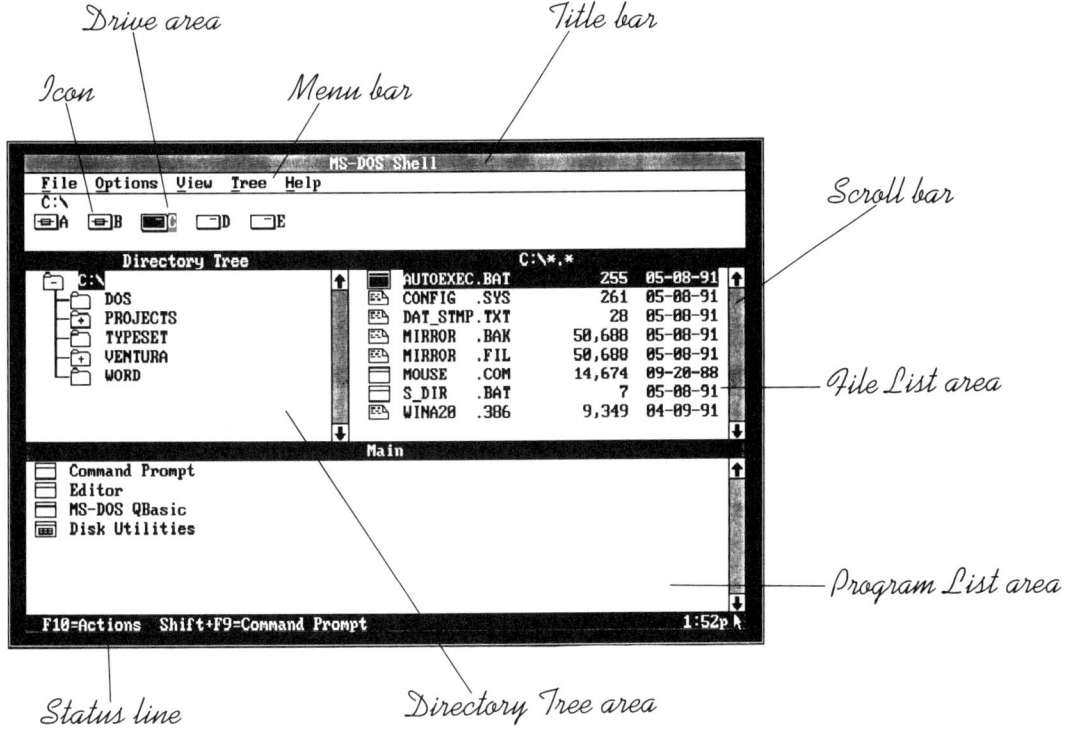

Drive area

Title bar

Icon

Menu bar

Scroll bar

File List area

Program List area

Status line

Directory Tree area

The screen above shows the Shell displayed on a VGA monitor in *graphics mode*. You can also display the Shell in *text mode*. What's the difference? In graphics mode, the screen is drawn pixel by pixel, or dot by dot, so DOS can display pictorial representations, called *icons*, of things like disk drives and file folders. In text mode, the screen is drawn with a predefined set of characters—letters, numbers, lines, and symbols—so DOS can't create such a fancy screen. All the screen illustrations in this book were created in graphics mode, and you shouldn't worry if your screen looks slightly different from ours. (See page 19 for instructions on how to switch between graphics and text modes.)

Graphics mode

Text mode

A Tour of the Shell

If you have worked with the Windows 3 File Manager or with programs for the Macintosh, many of the components of the DOS Shell will be familiar to you. Let's take a quick tour to make sure we are all speaking the same language. The Shell screen consists of the following:

The title bar   The words *MS-DOS Shell* in the title bar confirm that you are in the Shell.

The menu bar   Below the title bar, the menu bar displays the available menus: File, Options, View, Tree, and Help. (The Tree menu does not appear when the Program List area at the bottom of the screen is active.) The DOS commands are categorized and listed on these menus. We'll show you how to display menus and choose commands in a minute.

The drive area   This area displays the available drives. You might have only two drives in this area—C, which represents your hard drive, and A, which represents your floppy drive. If your hard disk is divided into sections, or *partitions*, you might have several drives available, one for each partition plus your floppy drive or drives. (See page 34 for more information about partitions.) Or, if you are working on a network, your screen might display the drives on other computers to which you have access. The active drive—in this case, drive C—is highlighted.

The display areas   DOS divides the rest of the screen into areas that display various kinds of information:

Directory Tree area

- The Directory Tree area, which displays a diagram of the directories on the selected drive. (We'll discuss directories in detail in the next chapter.) Because drive C is selected in the drive area, a diagram of the directories that branch off the drive C root directory is displayed in the Directory Tree area.

File List area

- The File List area, which displays the names of the files stored in the directory selected in the Directory Tree area. Currently, the File List area displays the names of the files stored in your root directory. (The notation *C:* in the area's title bar indicates that the list is for the root directory, and the notation *.* indicates that all the files in that directory are displayed.)

Program List area

- The Program List area, which displays the names of programs or groups of programs that have been assigned to this area. When you first start DOS, two groups appear: the Main group and the Disk Utilities group, which is a subgroup of Main. The name of the active group appears in the area's title bar. (See page 64 for more information about groups.)

The Shell can also display a fourth area called the Active Task List area, which allows you to switch between open applications. This area is displayed only when the Task Swapper is active. (See page 65 for more information about the Task Swapper.)

Scroll bars   You use the scroll bar to the right of each area to move through a list that is too long to fit in the area. If a list contains more items than can fit, the position of the small box in the scroll bar tells you approximately where you are in the list. (The box is at the top of the bar if you are at the top of the list, in the middle if you are in the middle, and so on.) You need a mouse to use the scroll bars to scroll the list. (We'll tell you how to scroll with the keyboard in a minute.)

The status line   DOS displays useful keyboard shortcuts, messages, and the current time in the status line.

The mouse pointer   If you have installed a mouse, you see the pointer in the Shell screen.

Moving Around the Shell

You can move from one Shell area to another using either the keyboard or the mouse. Some programs that rely heavily on visual ways of giving instructions, such as Windows applications and almost all Apple Macintosh programs, are cumbersome to use if you don't have a mouse. Not the DOS Shell. Although some tasks may be easier to carry out by pointing and clicking, those of you who would rather stick with the keyboard will still be able to move easily around the Shell screen. Here's how:

1. Press the Tab key to move clockwise from one area to the next. Press Shift-Tab to move counterclockwise.

   From area to area

2. When the title bar of the area you want is highlighted, indicating that it is active, use the Arrow keys to move from item to item within the area.

   From item to item

*Activating the
menu bar*

*Moving with a
mouse*

3. When the item you want is highlighted, activate the menu bar by pressing the Alt key. (We'll explain how to actually choose commands in a minute.)

4. Press Esc to move back to the Shell areas without choosing a command.

Now that the mouse users among you have a feel for how easy it is to get quickly where you want to go using the keyboard, let's see how to move around with the mouse. And it couldn't be easier! With the mouse, you don't have to first select the area you want to work in and then select the directory, file, or program you want to work with. Simply clicking the directory, file, or program both activates its area and highlights it.

Displaying Menus

As we have mentioned, in the Shell you tell DOS what you want to do with a highlighted item by choosing a command from a menu. Let's take a look at the menus now, first with the keyboard:

```
File
Open
Run...
Print
Associate...
Search...
View File Contents   F9

Move...              F7
Copy...              F8
Delete...            Del
Rename...
Change Attributes...

Create Directory...

Select All
Deselect All

Exit                 Alt+F4
```

1. To activate the menu bar, press the Alt key. DOS highlights the first menu name, File, and also highlights the first letters of the other four menus.

2. Press the F key to display the File menu, which lists the commands that perform file-related tasks.

3. Having displayed a menu, you can now press the Left and Right Arrow keys to display adjacent menus. For

---

Clicking

You click the left mouse button to select items, choose commands from menus, and select options. Clicking is a simple matter of pointing to an object and then pressing and releasing the mouse button once. ♦

Double-clicking

Double-clicking with the mouse involves pointing to an object and clicking the left mouse button twice in rapid succession. Double-clicking is used to start programs. You can also click a file to both load it and at the same time start the application program that created it. ♦

Scrolling

You can use several methods to scroll through long lists with scroll bars. Clicking the arrows at the bottom of the bars moves the contents a line at a time, and clicking on either side of the boxes in the scroll bars moves the contents a windowful at a time. You can also drag the scroll boxes up or down within the bar to move in the desired direction. ♦

example, press the Right Arrow key to close the File menu and display the Options menu, which lists commands that allow you to change the appearance of the Shell, change the way it displays files and directories, indicate whether you want to be prompted each time you are about to delete a file, and more.

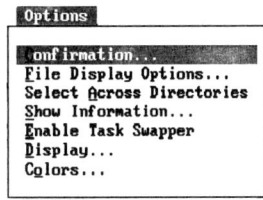

4. To close a menu without choosing a command, you press the Esc key. Close the Options menu now.

5. Next, hold down the Alt key and press the V key to display the View menu. (From now on, when we want you to hold down one key while pressing another, we'll indicate the action as *press Alt-V*.) The View menu lists commands that affect the way items are listed in the Shell areas on your screen.

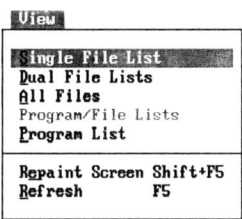

6. With the View menu still open, press the Right Arrow key to display the Tree menu, which includes commands to display more or less of the directory structure shown in the Directory Tree area.

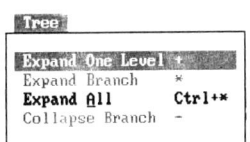

7. Close the Tree menu and leave the menu bar by pressing the Esc key.

You can open the remaining menu, Help, from the keyboard in the same way—by pressing Alt-H. However, if you have a mouse, try using it to display the Help menu:

1. No matter what area of the Shell is currently active, simply point to the name *Help* on the menu bar, and click the left mouse button.

2. To close the menu without choosing a command and without changing the active area, click the MS-DOS Shell title bar.

Choosing Commands

The best way to see how to choose a command from a menu is to actually do it, so follow along with this example. You'll not only learn how to give DOS instructions, but you'll also get a feel for how you can modify the Shell screen to display the same basic information in different ways. To explore some of these options, follow these steps:

1. Display the View menu, either by pressing Alt-V or by clicking the word *View* on the menu bar. Notice that the Program/File Lists command is dimmed. You can't

choose this command because this screen setup is already active.

2. The first command on the menu, Single File List, is highlighted. Let's see how this command affects the screen display. Press Enter or click this command to choose it. Your screen now looks something like this:

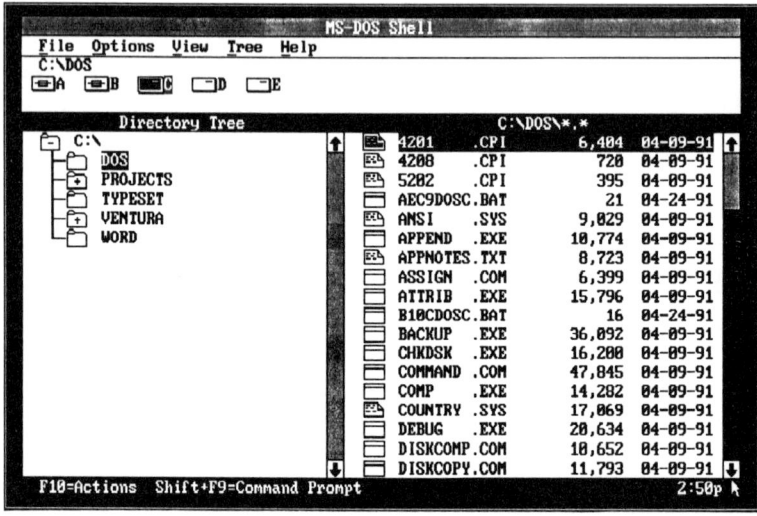

As you can see, the Program List area has disappeared and the Directory Tree and File List areas have expanded to take its place. If you have a lot of directories and files, you can see more directories and filenames without having to scroll.

3. From the View menu, choose the Dual File Lists command. DOS displays two Directory Tree and File List areas, allowing you to compare, copy, or move files between different directories or even between different drives. (We cover these tasks in Chapter 3.)

4. Next, from the View menu, choose the All Files command, which displays an alphabetical list of all the files on the selected drive, no matter what directory they are stored in. This command allows you to work with files from different directories at the same time and provides a powerful tool for reorganizing files.

5. From the View menu, choose the Program List command. DOS closes the Directory Tree and File List

areas, giving maximum space to the Program List area so that you can see the programs or groups of programs that you can run from the Shell.

6. Now, so that we are all working from the same screen, choose the Program/File Lists command from the View menu to restore the original view.

The remaining commands on the View menu, Repaint Screen and Refresh, affect updating of the Shell display. The Repaint Screen command redisplays the Shell screen if it didn't automatically redraw itself after you finished running a program from the Shell. The Refresh command tells the Shell to read all the files on the current drive and update its display if necessary. Sometimes when you create a file from within an application program, the file is not displayed when you return to the Shell until you use the Refresh commmand to display any new files.

Updating the Shell screen

From now on, we won't give step-by-step instructions for choosing commands. We'll simply say *choose this command from that menu* and leave it up to you whether you use the keyboard or a mouse.

Using Dialog Boxes

When DOS needs more information before it can carry out a command, it displays a special type of menu, called a *dialog box*, for you to fill in. You can tell ahead of time whether a dialog box will be displayed because commands that require

Menu conventions	**Changing the way files are displayed**	**Switching between text and graphics modes**
A dimmed command cannot be selected. If an ellipsis (...) follows the command name, a dialog box appears when you choose the command. A diamond preceding the command name indicates that the command is active. (Commands that flip, or toggle, between active and inactive states use this convention.) ♦	You can display lists of files in ascending or descending order by name, extension, date, size, or diskorder. (Diskorder is the order in which files were put on the disk). Choose File Display Options from the Options menu, and select the option you want. ♦	You can change the screen display from text to graphics modes and vice versa by choosing the Display command from the Options menu. Two graphics modes and two text modes are listed. You can preview the effects of any changes you make by selecting the Preview command button. ♦

more information have an ellipsis (...) after their names on the menu. Dialog boxes are an important component of the Shell. Let's take a look at a typical dialog box:

1. From the Options menu, choose the File Display Options command to display the following File Display Options dialog box:

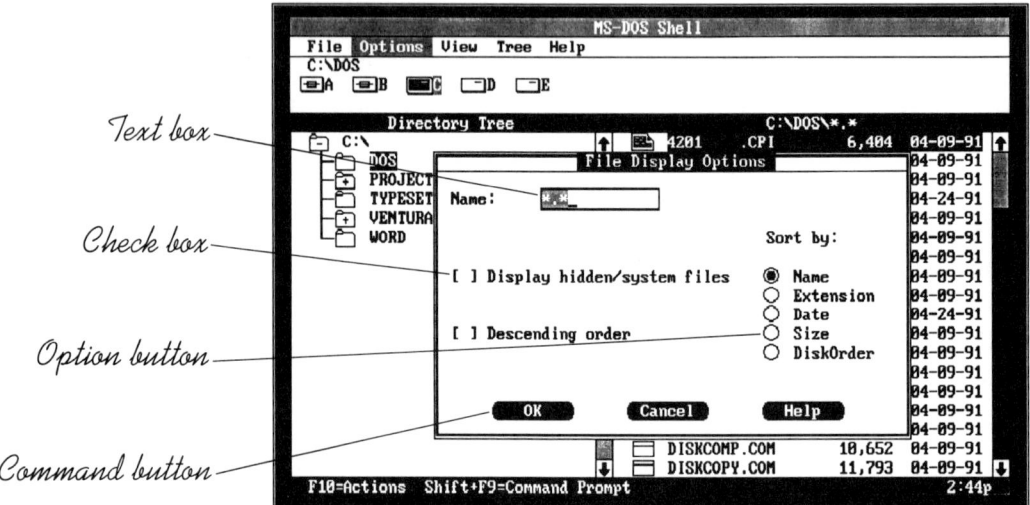

Text box

Check box

Option button

Command button

Like this example, dialog boxes can have one or more of the following:

Text boxes   You type information, such as a filename that DOS needs to carry out a command, in text boxes.

List boxes   DOS displays items such as filenames in list boxes. (The Display Options dialog box does not include an example of a list box.) List boxes resemble the File List area of the Shell screen. You can sometimes select more than one item from a list box, and if a list contains more items than can be displayed at one time, you can scroll out-of-sight items into view by pressing the Up and Down Arrow keys or by using the mouse in the list box's scroll bar.

Option buttons   Groups of small, round buttons. Mutually exclusive—you can select only one option from a group of option buttons. For example, in the File Display Options dialog box, you can specify only one method of sorting files. A black dot indicates which option is selected.

Check boxes Square buttons. Not mutually exclusive—you can select any number of check boxes. For example, in the File Display Options dialog box, you can select both the Display Hidden/System Files and the Descending Order options. An X indicates which check boxes are selected.

Command buttons You use command buttons to tell DOS to carry out the command (OK), cancel the command (Cancel), or help you use the command (Help). Dialog boxes may have other command buttons, depending on the needs of the command.

Moving around a dialog box is easy. With the keyboard:

Moving around a dialog box

- To move the highlight from area to area in a dialog box, use the Tab key.
- To enter information in a text box, highlight the text box, and begin typing.

Using text boxes

- To select an option from a list or an option-button group, use the Arrow keys.

Selecting options

- To select a check box, move the highlight to the check box, and press the Spacebar. Pressing the Spacebar when an X appears in a check box, indicating that it is already selected, clears the box and deselects the option.

Selecting check boxes

- To select a command button, move the highlight to the button, and press the Enter key.

Selecting command buttons

With a mouse, you select items from lists, option buttons, check boxes, and command buttons by clicking them. We will practice using dialog boxes in Chapter 3.

Getting Help in the Shell

Using the Shell is fairly intuitive, and this book will help you find your way around so that, most of the time, you will know exactly what to do and how. However, for those times when you stumble over a particular operation, DOS provides an excellent Help feature. Think of the Help feature as another book that you can page through for help.

You access the Help feature by choosing one of the following commands from the Help menu:

Help menu

- The Index command gives you a broad view of the topics available.

- The Keyboard command displays a list of keyboard shortcuts for working in the Shell.
- The Shell Basics command gives a brief overview of how to use the Shell.
- The Commands command lists the available commands by menu and gives a brief explanation of each one.
- The Procedures command gives instructions for performing common procedures.
- The Using Help command gives instructions for using the Help feature.
- The About Shell command gives copyright and version information.

Let's take a look at a Help screen to get you oriented, and then we'll leave you to explore the Help feature on your own:

1. From the Help menu, choose the Commands command. This Help screen appears, showing a list of menus arranged by Shell area:

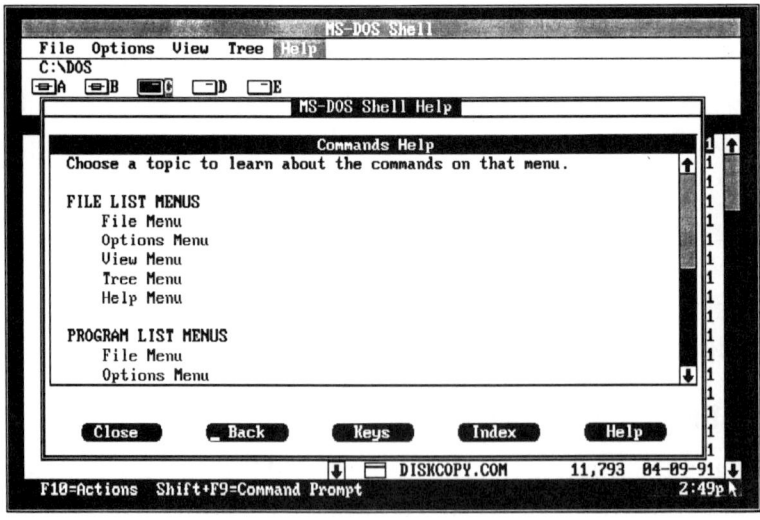

2. Press the Tab key until View Menu under FILE LIST MENUS is highlighted, and then press Enter. (With a mouse, you can simply double-click View Menu.) DOS displays a list of the commands on the View menu:

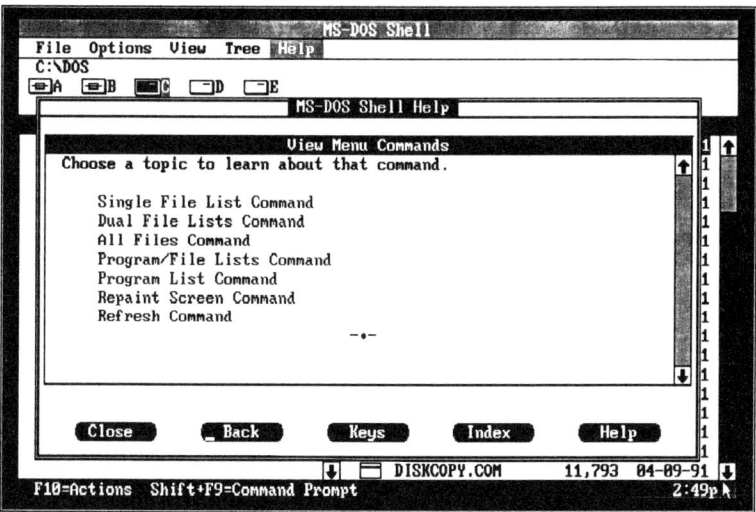

3. Press Tab to highlight All Files Command, and press Enter. (Again, with a mouse you can double-click All Files Command.) An explanation of the All Files command appears:

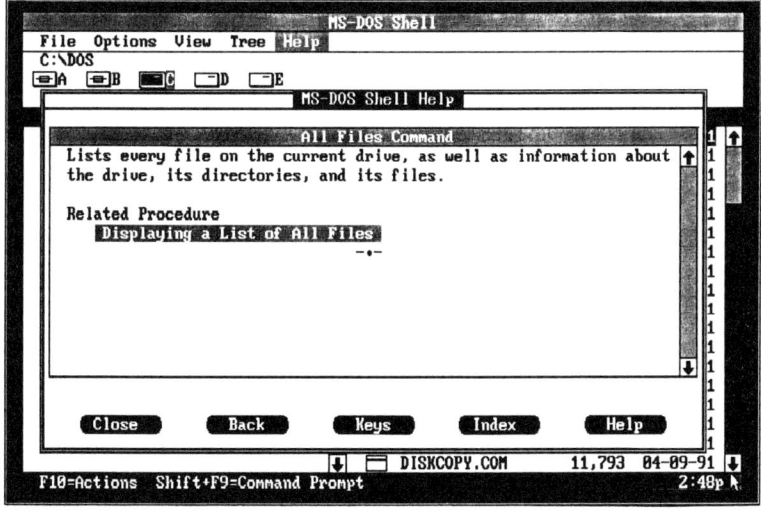

4. Press Tab to move the highlight to the Close command button.
5. At this point, you can press Enter to leave (close) Help, or press Tab to move to one of the other command buttons. Selecting Back takes you back to the previous Help screen, selecting Keys takes you to the set of screens you see if you choose the Keyboard command from the Help menu, selecting Index takes you to the

set of screens you see if you choose the Index command, and selecting Help offers further information. For now, press Enter to close the dialog box.

Help shortcut

You can also get help with a specific command by highlighting the command on its menu and pressing F1. For example, if you press Alt-V to open the View menu and then use the Down Arrow key to move the highlight to the All Files command, pressing F1 displays the Help screen shown on the previous page.

That concludes our brief overview of the Shell. Before we move on to discuss working on the command line, we need to talk about ways of moving between the two sides of DOS.

Moving Between the Shell and the Command Line

Exiting the Shell

As you know, to start the Shell you type *dosshell*. To leave the Shell, you can either press F3 or choose Exit from the File menu. Both of these actions terminate the Shell program, remove the Shell from memory, and display the command prompt, which usually looks like this:

   C:\\>

or this:

   C>

To reload the Shell, you simply enter *dosshell* again.

Displaying the command prompt

If you usually work in the Shell but you want to temporarily display the command prompt so that you can enter a command that is not available from within the Shell, you can press Shift-F9 or select Command Prompt from the Program List area. In either case, DOS displays the command prompt, and your screen looks as it does when you exit the Shell. But in fact, the Shell is still loaded. Pressing Shift-F9 or selecting Command Prompt loads an additional copy of COMMAND.COM on top of the existing copy, enabling you to enter commands without exiting the Shell. You then type *exit* and press Enter at the command prompt to quit the second copy of COMMAND.COM and return to the Shell. Let's do it now:

1. With the Shell on your screen, press Shift-F9, or double-click Command Prompt in the Program List area.
2. At the command prompt, type *dir* (for *directory*), and press Enter. DOS displays a list of the directories and files in the root directory.
3. Type *exit* and press Enter to return to the Shell.

If you type *dosshell* instead of *exit*, you load a second copy of the Shell and take up memory unnecessarily. If you are at the command prompt and you can't remember whether you actually quit the Shell to get there or just loaded another copy of COMMAND.COM, simply type *exit* and press Enter. It won't hurt anything if you did quit the Shell, and if you loaded a second copy of COMMAND.COM, you will return to the Shell.

Now quit the Shell entirely so that we can get on with our discussion of the command line:

1. Press F3 to quit the Shell.

The Command Line

When you are working at the command line, your screen shows only the command prompt. When this prompt is displayed, DOS is waiting for you to type a command at the cursor, which is usually a blinking underscore to the right of the prompt. When you type a command, DOS springs into action. For example, if you type

ver

(for *version*) and press Enter, DOS displays its version number and then redisplays the command prompt.

Command Syntax

To run a command from the command line, you have to type its name, and you may have to type *parameters* and *switches*. These are the equivalent of the additional information you give in dialog boxes in the Shell. Some commands take no parameters or switches. For example, you can simply type *mem* and press Enter to have DOS display a report of your computer's memory configuration.

Parameters   Parameters are the equivalent of information you type in text boxes in Shell dialog boxes. Some commands require parameters. For example, if you type

copy

and press Enter, DOS responds with the message *Required parameter missing*, because DOS needs to know what you want to copy and where you want to copy it to in order to carry out the command. You must type something like

copy jones.doc a:

which means *copy the file called JONES.DOC to the floppy disk in the A drive.*

Switches   Switches are the equivalent of the option buttons and check boxes you select in Shell dialog boxes. Some commands have no switches, some have a few, and others have many. Switches modify the way a command performs its task. You enter a switch on the command line as a forward slash (/) followed by a single letter or number. For example, if you type

dir

DOS lists the names of the directories and files in the root directory, together with additional information such as their size and creation dates. (We talk more about the **dir** command on page 118.) If, on the other hand, you type

dir /w

DOS displays a wide listing that includes only the names of the directories and files, without any additional information.

Syntax diagrams   Because each command is different, both in its general structure and in the number of parameters and switches it has, we need a concise way of summarizing that information for each command. The summary is called a *syntax diagram*. You can display the syntax diagram for any command by typing the name of the command followed by /? and pressing Enter. Try it now:

Displaying a command's syntax

1.   At the command prompt, type *find /?* and press Enter. DOS displays the syntax diagram for the **find** command, like this:

```
C:\>find /?
Searches for a text string in a file or files.

FIND [/V] [/C] [/N] [/I] "string" [[drive:][path]filename[ ...]]

   /V        Displays all lines NOT containing the specified string.
   /C        Displays only the count of lines containing the string.
   /N        Displays line numbers with the displayed lines.
   /I        Ignores the case of characters when searching for the string.
   "string"  Specifies the text string to find.
   [drive:][path]filename
             Specifies a file or files to search.

If a pathname is not specified, FIND searches the text typed at the prompt
or piped from another command.

C:\>
```

Take heart: Syntax diagrams aren't really as baffling as they first appear. The syntax diagram for the **find** command tells us that the command has the following components:

- The command name—**find**.
- Four optional switches—[/v], [/c], [/n], and [/i].
- A required parameter—*"string"*.
- And four more parameters that are optional—[*drive*:], [*path*], [*filename*], and [...]. The optional parameter [...] indicates that you can include several parameters identical to the preceding one (*filename*).

(For more specific information about the syntax of this particular command, see page 124.)

Remember the following conventions when reading syntax diagrams:

Reading syntax diagrams

- Square brackets ([]) mean that the parameter or switch they enclose is optional. Type only the options you want, and *don't* type the brackets.
- An ellipsis (...) means you can repeat the preceding parameter. In most cases, the number of times you can repeat the parameter is limited by the maximum length of the command line (127 characters).
- A pipe symbol (|)—not present in the syntax diagram for the **find** command—indicates that the option preceding it and the option following it are mutually exclusive. Think of the pipe symbol as the word *or*.

- Spaces separate commands from their parameters and switches. Type the spaces where indicated.

Two additional conventions apply to printed syntax diagrams (like those in Chapter 6 of this book and in the documentation):

- Bold means you must type the item (for example, the command name) for the command to work. You can type it in either uppercase or lowercase letters.
- Italic means you replace the item with your own information; for example, the name of the file you want the command to operate on.

Admittedly, syntax diagrams can be a bit puzzling at first, but with a little practice, you will easily be able to make sense of them.

The command line is a picky taskmaster. Learning to use DOS commands is easier than learning a foreign language, but you shouldn't expect to become proficient overnight. The DOS Shell may ease this learning process, and, if you need to use only the basic DOS commands, you might be able to use the Shell for most of your work. If, however, you want to be a fluent speaker of DOS, spend some time puzzling out syntax diagrams and learning commands. Many of the DOS commands are not on the Shell menus, and although you can run most of these commands from within the Shell (by choosing Run from the File menu—see page 35), you need to know the name and syntax of the command.

Changing Your Default Working Environment

If you see the command prompt on your screen when you turn on your computer but, as a result of this tour of the Shell and the command line, you have decided you would prefer to use the Shell, you can set up your system so that DOS loads the Shell every time you start your computer. Similarly, if your computer loads the Shell when you turn it on but you would prefer to work on the command line, you can easily tell DOS not to load the Shell.

Changing the default working environment from the command line to the Shell (or vice versa) involves modifying your AUTOEXEC.BAT file, so for those of you who have never made the acquaintance of this file before, we'll digress here to explain what AUTOEXEC.BAT is and what it does.

The AUTOEXEC.BAT File

Your AUTOEXEC.BAT file is a collection of ordinary DOS commands that DOS executes every time you turn on your computer, just as if you had typed them at the command prompt. If you didn't have an AUTOEXEC.BAT file before DOS 5 was installed on your machine, the file was created during the installation process and placed in your root directory. If you did have an AUTOEXEC.BAT file, the installation program modified the file as necessary for DOS 5 to run smoothly.

Let's use the Editor provided with DOS to take a look at the contents of your AUTOEXEC.BAT file.

1. If the Shell is not displayed on your screen, type *dosshell* at the DOS prompt. In the drive area below the menu bar, check that your C drive is active (select it if it isn't) and that the C:\ at the top of the Directory Tree area is highlighted.

2. Press the Tab key to activate the Program List area, then use the Down Arrow key to highlight Editor, and press Enter. (With a mouse, double-click Editor in the Program List area.) This dialog box appears:

Loading the DOS Editor

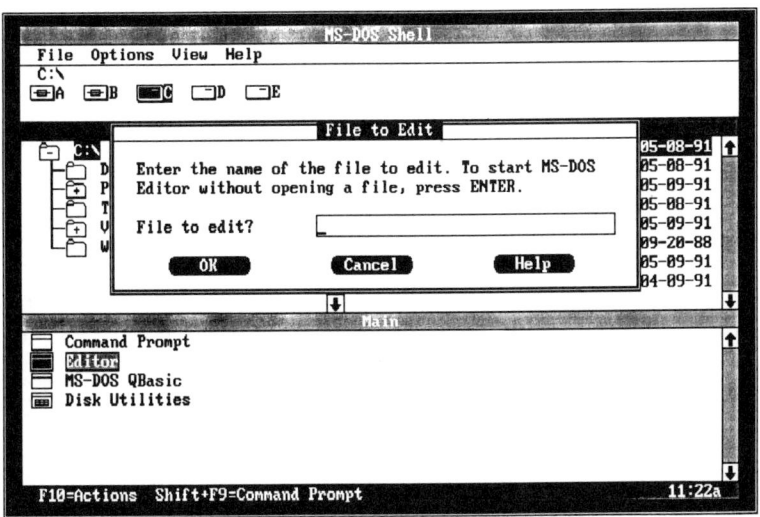

3. Type *AUTOEXEC.BAT* in the text box to indicate that you want to edit this file, and press Enter or click OK. The Shell screen is replaced by the DOS Editor screen, which displays the contents of the AUTOEXEC.BAT file. Your screen now looks similiar to this one:

4. Choose the Save As command from the File menu, type *AUTOEXEC.OLD* in the text box, and press Enter. Now choose the Open command from the File menu, type *AUTOEXEC.BAT* in the text box, and press Enter. These extremely important steps save a copy of your current AUTOEXEC.BAT file with a new name and reload the file named AUTOEXEC.BAT. If you have difficulty booting your computer after modifying the AUTOEXEC.BAT file, you'll be able to rename AUTOEXEC.OLD as AUTOEXEC.BAT and put everything back as it was. (We discuss renaming files on page 51.)

The path command

If you take a look at the AUTOEXEC.BAT file in the illustration above, you'll notice a **path** command, which specifies the directories DOS is to look in when you type the name of a command. Without a path, DOS looks only in the current directory. The **path** command in the illustration tells DOS to look in three directories: C:\ (the root directory), C:\DOS (the DOS directory), and C:\WORD (the WORD directory).

The prompt command

The illustration also shows a **prompt** command, which modifies the appearance of the command prompt. We talk more about this command on page 43.

Modifying the AUTOEXEC.BAT File

The Shell appears on your screen when you turn on your computer if your AUTOEXEC.BAT file contains the **dosshell** command. Otherwise, the command prompt appears on your screen. If you want to make the Shell your default environment, you need to add the **dosshell** command to your AUTOEXEC.BAT file, like this.:

1. Press Ctrl-End to move to the end of the file.
2. Type *dosshell*. Your AUTOEXEC.BAT now looks something like this:

The dosshell command

```
┌──────────────────────────────────────────────────────────┐
│ File  Edit  Search  Options                          Help │
│                   ┌─ AUTOEXEC.BAT ─┐                       │
│ @ECHO OFF                                                ↑ │
│ PROMPT $p$g                                                │
│ PATH C:\;C:\DOS;C:\WORD                                    │
│ SET TEMP=C:\DOS                                            │
│ MOUSE                                                      │
│ C:\DOS\mirror                                              │
│ dosshell                                                   │
│                                                           ↓ │
│ ←                                                        → │
│ MS-DOS Editor  <F1=Help> Press ALT to activate menus  00007:009 │
└──────────────────────────────────────────────────────────┘
```

3. Save the change by choosing Save from the File menu.
4. Select Exit from the File menu to quit the DOS Editor.

Editor requirements

The DOS Editor depends on the QBASIC.EXE file in your DOS directory. This file was copied to your hard disk when DOS was installed. If you move or delete the file, you will not be able to use the DOS Editor. To copy the QBASIC.EXE file back to your hard disk from the original DOS disks, you must use the **expand** command (see page 122). ♦

The top ten

Some DOS commands are especially suited for use in AUTOEXEC.BAT. The following list offers suggestions for commands that you might want to include in your AUTOEXEC.BAT file.

1. **path**
2. **prompt**
3. **chkdsk**
4. **mirror**
5. **set**
6. **cls**
7. **dosshell**
8. **date**
9. **time**
10. **break**

Check this book's index to see where you can find more information about each of these commands. ♦

*Deleting
dosshell*

If your computer boots with the Shell loaded and you want to work on the command line, follow these steps:

1. Use the Arrow keys to move to the line containing the **dosshell** command.
2. Press Ctrl-Y to delete the entire line.
3. Save the change by choosing Save from the File menu.
4. Select Exit from the File menu to quit the DOS Editor.

That's all there is to it! The next time you boot your computer, you will be in your chosen working environment.

In this chapter, we have shown you two ways to give commands to DOS, and you've taken a quick tour of the Shell and the command line. In the Shell, you've learned how to move around, how to choose commands, and how to give DOS all the information it needs to carry out your instructions. And you now know what your AUTOEXEC.BAT file is, what it looks like, and how to modify it in the DOS Editor. In the next chapter, we look at the workhorse DOS commands: those for creating directories, copying files, renaming files, and carrying out other common tasks.

3

Managing Your Files

Some people work efficiently in the midst of chaos. Even when surrounded by piles of paper, they can always lay their hands on exactly what they need at any given moment. Similarly, some people store all their electronic files in their computer's root directory, yet they know which files relate to which project or client account, and they have no difficulty retrieving the document they need from a seemingly random assortment.

And then there are the rest of us. We keep the manilla-file-folder manufacturers in business and color-code everything in our attempts to keep from drowning in paper. Organizing our electronic files is no less crucial to our efficiency and peace of mind than organizing our paper files.

DOS can be a big help when it comes to organizing files. With commands like **md** (Make Directory), **copy**, **ren** (Rename), and **del** (Delete), DOS can help you wrestle order out of chaos. And when you use DOS to create the equivalent of an electronic filing cabinet, you will be pleased to discover that you can manipulate whole categories of files just as easily as you can mainipulate one file at a time.

Working with Drives, Directories, and Files

Organizing your files on the computer is a simple matter of dividing them into logical groups. Electronically, this division takes place on three levels: drives, directories, and files.

Creating and Naming Drives

Hard-disk partitions

If you have worked with computers for a while, you are probably familiar with the concept of *partitioning*, or dividing, a hard disk into areas known as *drives*. Hard-disk partitioning was used often with versions of DOS earlier than DOS 4, because those versions allowed you to use hard-disk storage areas of up to only 32 MB. If you had a hard disk that was larger than 32 MB, to make best use of it you had to partition your hard disk into chunks of 32 MB or less. With DOS 5, the partition size is 2 gigabytes—no longer a limiting factor for most people.

If your hard disk is not currently partitioned, we suggest that you use directories to divide your disk space instead of drives. If your hard disk is partitioned, you see drives for each partition in the drive area of the DOS Shell screen. Traditionally, if you have only one drive, it is called drive C, and if you have several drives, they are assigned consecutive letters—D, E, and so on. Also by tradition, the drive letters A and B are reserved for floppy drives.

In addition to letter names, drives can also have *volume labels*. These labels are usually assigned to floppy disks to give a general idea of the disk's contents. For example, you might assign the volume label ACCOUNTS90 to a floppy disk containing an archive of last year's accounting information, to distinguish it from similar information for other years. You can also assign labels to hard drives.

Volume labels

To assign a volume label, you enter the **label** command on the command line. Follow these steps:

1. If you are in the Shell, choose the Run command from the File menu. (When you want to enter only one command, choosing Run is often quicker than pressing Shift-F9 to load another copy of COMMAND.COM.) If you are at the command prompt, skip this step.

The Run command

2. Type *label*, and press Enter. DOS displays the following message:

```
Volume in drive C has no label
Volume Serial Number is 168F-6897
Volume label (11 characters, ENTER for none)?
```

3. Type a label for your C drive, and press Enter. (Press Enter twice if you used the Run command.)

To delete a volume label, use the **label** command again, this time pressing Enter without typing a name. Confirm the deletion by typing *y* and pressing Enter when prompted.

Creating and Naming Directories

As you know, divisions within drives are called *directories*. Every drive has a root directory, from which all other directories branch. Subdirectories can branch from directories, and so on. (In this book, we use the term *directory* to mean any directory other than the root directory, using the term *subdirectory* only when the relationship between directories is important.)

Creating directories is quick and easy, so never hesitate if a new directory will help you better organize your files. Before you create your first directory, however, you should give some thought to the kind of hierarchy you want to create. Should you create application-program directories that branch from the root directory (such as C:\WORD for your word processor) and then create subdirectories within those program directories (such as C:\WORD\LETTERS and C:\WORD\REPORTS)? Or is it more logical to create client directories that branch from the root directory (such as C:\SUNCRAFT) and then create subdirectories within those client directories (such as C:\SUNCRAFT\LETTERS and C:\SUNCRAFT\REPORTS)?

The nature of your work will probably determine how you set up your directories. Just be sure that you have a system of some kind.

To see how easy it is to create directories, follow along with a few examples. First, use the Shell to create a new directory that branches from the root directory:

1. With the Shell displayed on your screen, the Directory Tree area active, and C:\ (the root directory) selected, choose the Create Directory command from the File menu. The Create Directory dialog box appears:

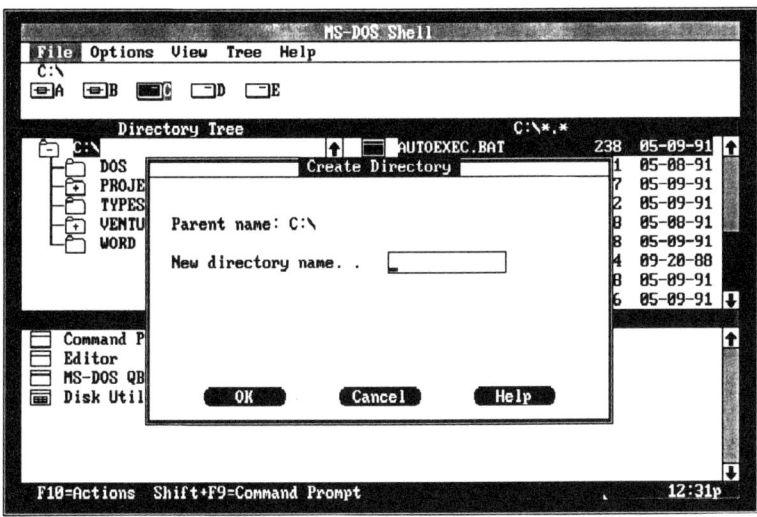

2. Type *backup* in the text box, and press Enter. The newly created BACKUP directory shows up in the Directory Tree area as a new directory branching from the root directory:

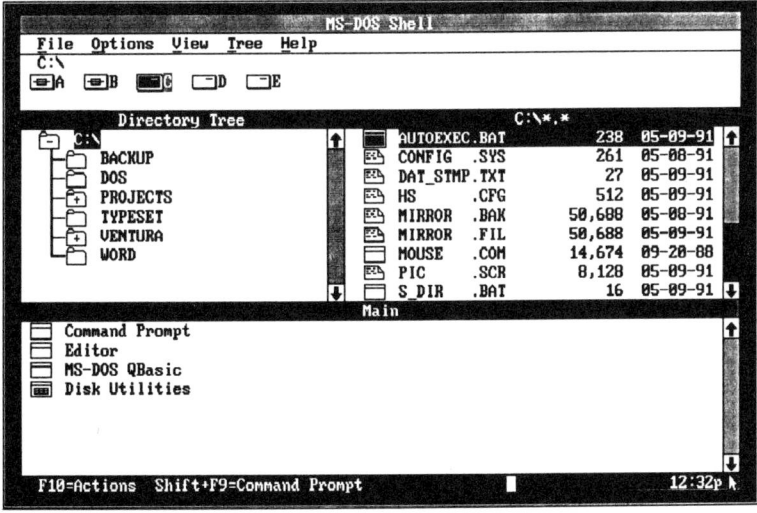

Now let's create another directory, but this time from the command line. To create a directory, you use the **md** (Make Directory) command, as follows:

1. Display the command prompt by pressing Shift-F9.

2. Type *md basic*, and press Enter to create the C:\BASIC directory. Nothing appears to happen, but behind the scenes, DOS has followed your orders and created a BASIC directory.

Entering the md command

3. Type *exit*, and press Enter to return to the Shell. Where is the new directory? The Shell screen looks exactly as it did when you left it. To see the new directory, you have to update the screen.

Updating the Shell screen

4. Choose the Refresh command from the View menu to update the Shell screen. Now you see the new directory.

Later in this chapter, we'll move all the Basic files that are currently stored in the DOS directory into both the BASIC and BACKUP directories, so for the time being, don't erase these empty directories.

Creating and Naming Files

Files can be divided into two main catagories: program files and data files.

Program files contain instructions to the computer. Unlike data files (described next) which you create, program files are usually created by programmers to run applications, such as Microsoft Word or Quattro Pro.

Data files are files you create while running an application program. An example is a letter you create using a word processor, such as WordPerfect. The simplest type of data file is an *unformatted file*, which contains only text and/or numbers. The data files you create when you work with most application programs are composed of text, numbers, and formatting instructions specific to the program with which

Unformatted files

ASCII files	Filenames	Directory names
Unformatted files are often referred to as ASCII (pronounced *askey*) files, because they are stored by the computer as ASCII codes. (ASCII stands for American Standard Code for Information Interchange.) You don't need to know anything about these codes, but you now know that the term *ASCII file* simply means an unformatted file. ♦	A filename is made up of two parts, the name and the extension, separated by a period. Names cannot be more than eight characters, and extensions cannot be more than three characters. They can both consist of letters, numbers, and these characters: _^$!#%&-{}() They cannot contain spaces, commas, or periods. ♦	Directory names can also be made up of a name and an extension. They are subject to the same eight-character limit for the name and the same three-character limit for the extension. The extension is often omitted from directory names to more easily distinguish them from filenames. ♦

you created the file. These files are known as *formatted files* because of the formatting instructions that create such elements as bold or italic type, centered text, and so on.

Formatted files

Before launching into a discussion of how to organize files, we need to cover some basics about assigning names to data files, because how you name your files can have an impact on your ability to manipulate them efficiently.

Whether you work alone or with others, and whether you work on your own computer or share a machine with colleagues, you should have a file-naming system that allows you to do the following:

File-naming system

- Predict what the name of a file will be, based on a few facts about the file's contents.
- Remember what is in a file—even a couple of months after you create it—based on its name.
- Manipulate several files using only one command, because their filenames are similar (more about this later).

File-naming conventions don't need to be complicated—in fact, the simpler the better. All you need is a systematic way of naming files. For example, a small company might keep a set of three files containing salary, pension, and benefit information for each employee. The first three characters of the filename might represent the category (*sal*, *pen*, *ben*), the next three characters might represent the employee's initials, and the last two characters might be reserved for the year. Typical filenames might look something like these:

penssw89.doc

penssw90.doc

Notice that the eight characters allowed by DOS for filenames are all used in these examples, because files are sometimes easier to manipulate if you know that they are all the same length. Also notice that particular information is specified in a particular order, giving the filenames a consistent structure and allowing you to select groups of files to be used with DOS commands. We discuss how you make these selections next.

Making File Selections

The first step in getting electronically organized is knowing how to select files so that you can arrange them logically.

Selecting Drives and Directories

The Shell really shines when it comes to displaying drive information and enabling you to move easily between directories. Let's put the Shell through its paces. Recall from Chapter 2 that the Shell displays each of your available drives in a row below the menu bar. Here's how you switch drives:

Switching drives in the Shell

1. Select the drive you want to switch to by tabbing to the drive area, using the Left and Right Arrow keys to highlight the drive, and pressing Enter, or by clicking the drive with the mouse.

The Directory Tree area now shows a diagram of the directories on the selected drive. To move to a particular directory:

Switching directories in the Shell

1. Tab to the Directory Tree area, and use the Up and Down Arrow keys to select a directory icon, or click the directory icon with the mouse.

The Shell then displays the names of the files in that directory in the File List area. For example, here's the result after we reselected drive C and then selected the C:\DOS directory in the Directory Tree area:

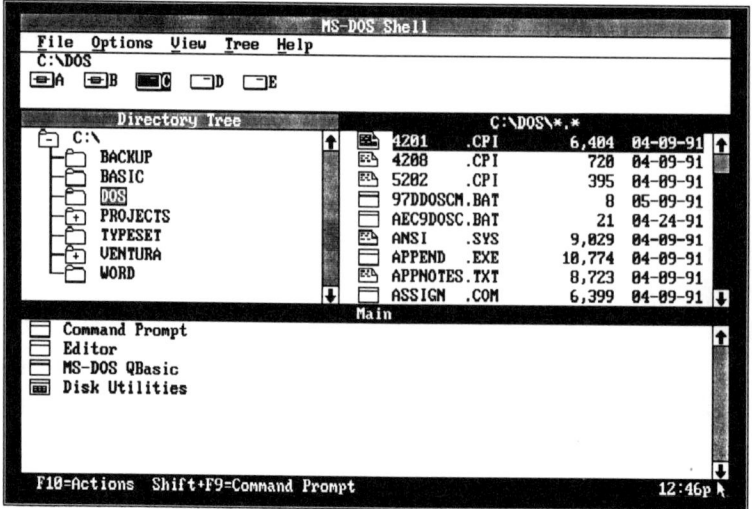

You might notice that some of the names in the Directory Tree area have a plus (+) sign. The plus sign indicates that the directory has at least one subdirectory. To display subdirectories:

1. Select the directory.
2. Expand the directory by pressing the + key or by clicking the plus sign.

Expanding a directory

When you expand a directory, the plus sign changes to a minus (–) sign, like this:

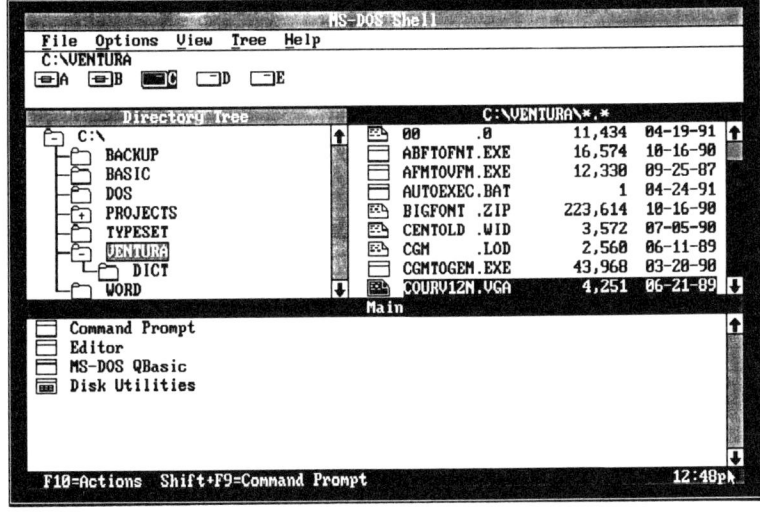

To hide subdirectories:

1. Select the directory containing the subdirectories.
2. Collapse the directory by pressing the minus (-) key or by clicking the minus sign.

Collapsing a directory

Now let's see how you switch drives and directories from the command line:

1. Press Shift-F9 to display the command prompt.
2. Type the letter of the drive you want followed by a colon, and press Enter. For example, insert a disk in your floppy drive, type *a:*, and press Enter to activate that drive.

Switching drives on the command line

3. Type *c:*, and press Enter to switch back to drive C.

Moving between directories on the command line is a bit more involved. You use the **cd** (Change Directory) command, followed by the path of the directory to which you want to move. (As explained in Chapter 2, the path is the trail DOS must follow through the directory tree to find the directory.) To try switching directories, follow these steps:

Entering the cd command

1. Type *cd c:\dos* and press Enter to move to the DOS directory.
2. Type *cd c:\basic*, and press Enter to move to the BASIC directory.
3. Return to the C:\DOS directory by typing *cd c:\dos* and pressing Enter.

Switching shortcuts

So far, you've switched to a directory by using its full path. Under certain circumstances, you can use shortcuts to switch directories. To understand when you can use shortcuts, take a look at this diagram:

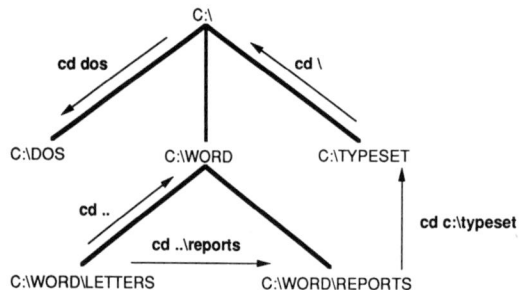

To move from the C:\ directory to the C:\DOS subdirectory, you can use the shortcut

cd dos

To move from the C:\WORD\REPORTS subdirectory up one level in the directory hierarchy to C:\WORD (known as *moving to the parent directory*), you can use the shortcut

cd ..

The two periods mean *No matter where I am, take me up one level*. To move from the C:\WORD\LETTERS subdirectory to the C:\WORD\REPORTS subdirectory, you can use the shortcut

cd ..\reports

Finally, to move from anywhere in the directory hierarchy to the root directory, you can use the shortcut

**cd **

To move anywhere else in the directory structure, you must use the **cd** command with the full path of the directory to which you want to move. So, for example, to move from the C:\WORD\REPORTS subdirectory to the C:\TYPESET directory, you must enter

cd c:\typeset

Keeping Track of Where You Are

The default command prompt is simply the letter of the current drive (for example, C>). You can use the **prompt** command to change the command prompt so that it includes the path of the directory you are currently in. Then, if you move from the root directory to the C:\WORD\LETTERS directory, the command prompt becomes

C:\WORD\LETTERS>

You never have to wonder where you are in the hierarchy. A quick look at the command prompt gets you oriented.

If the installation program created your AUTOEXEC.BAT file when you installed DOS 5, you probably see the path as part of your command prompt. If you don't see it, add the path to your command prompt by following these steps:

1. On the command line, type *prompt*, a space, and *$p*.
2. To follow the prompt with a right angle bracket, type *$g*. The command now looks like this:

   prompt pg
3. Press Enter.
4. Type *cd * and press Enter to move to the root directory, and then type *cd dos* and press Enter to move to the DOS directory. Notice how the command prompt reflects your current position in the directory hierarchy.

Adding the path to the prompt

To always display the path in the command prompt, add the **prompt** command to your AUTOEXEC.BAT file. See page 29 for instructions on how to modify this file.

Viewing Directory Contents

So now you know how to navigate to a specific directory. If you are working from the Shell, a list of the files in that directory is automatically displayed in the File List area. If you are working from the command line, you can display the directory's contents by using the **dir** command. Here's how:

1. Enter *dir* to see a complete listing of the files in the DOS directory.

Did the files scroll by too quickly for you to see all of them? You can display the listing one screenful at a time.

Viewing a screenful of files

1. Enter *dir /p* (think of /p as *pause* or *page*).
2. This time DOS lists all the filenames that will fit on one screen. Press any key to see the next screenful of files.

If all you want to do is check a filename or two, you can tell DOS to pack the filenames on the screen, like this:

Viewing only filenames

1. Enter *dir /w* (think of /w as *wide*). DOS lists the filenames (without date, time, and size information) across the screen in rows.
2. Type *exit* and press Enter to return to the Shell.

Understanding what you see   When you enter *dir* to see a listing of files, you see a display something like this one:

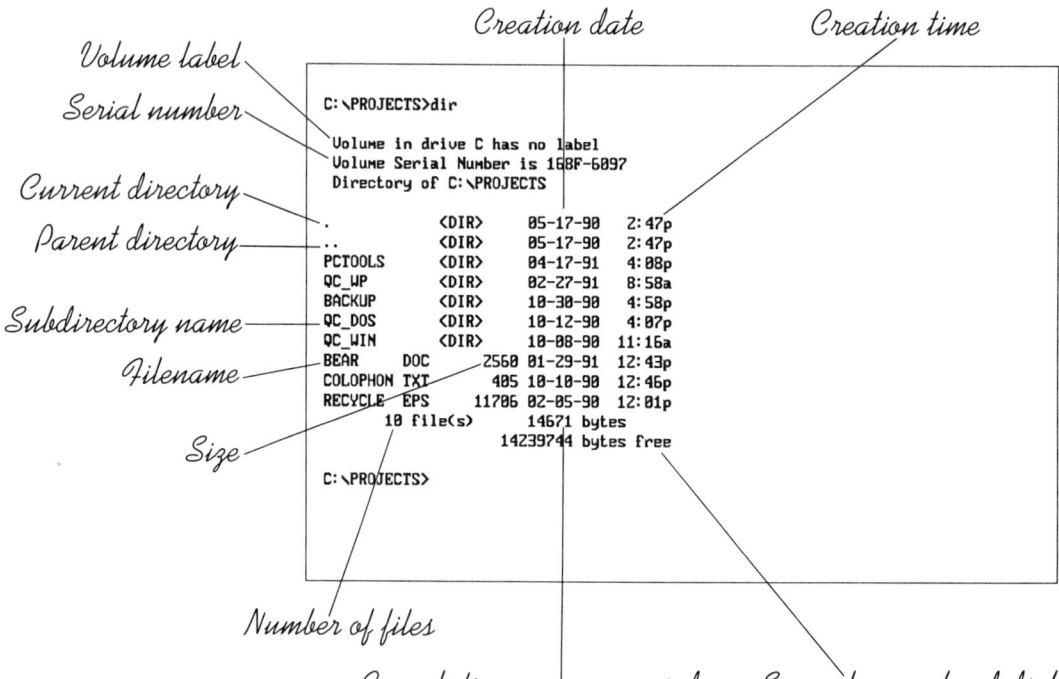

Creation date   *Creation time*

Volume label

Serial number

Current directory

Parent directory

Subdirectory name

Filename

Size

Number of files

Cumulative space occupied   *Space free on hard disk*

DOS always prefaces the list with the volume label and the serial number of the disk. In all subdirectory listings, these entries are followed by a . (one period), which refers to the current directory, and .. (two periods), which refers to the parent directory (the directory one level up in the hierarchy). These entries are listed even if the directory contains no files. If you request a listing of a directory that contains sub-directories, you then see files and directories in what appears to be random order. In fact, the files and directories are listed in the order in which they were created. The names of the subdirectories are followed by <DIR> and their date and time of creation, and the names of the files are followed by their size and date and time of creation. Finally, at the end of the directory, DOS tells you how many files are in the directory, how many bytes of space all the files take up, and how much free space is available on the drive.

Selecting Files

If you are working in the Shell, you can use several methods to select files. If you are working on the command line, you can either select files one at a time or use characters known as *wildcards* to select groups of files. (You can also use wildcards in the Shell.) We'll cover all of these methods here.

Using wildcards to display files   The beauty of consistent filenames becomes apparent when you need to do something with several files as a group (such as moving all files that have 90 as the last two characters of their filenames.) The key to selecting groups of files is knowing how to use the DOS wildcard characters: the asterisk (*) and the question mark (?).

- Use the asterisk to represent groups of characters or even entire names and extensions.
- Use the question mark to specify a single character.

Representing filenames with wildcard characters is a powerful technique. Try it now, by displaying all the files in the DOS directory that have an EXE extension:

1. In the Directory Tree area, select the DOS directory.
2. From the Options menu, choose File Display Options.
3. Notice that the Name text box shows *.* as the default selection, meaning that all files in the DOS directory, no matter what their filenames and extensions, are currently displayed in the File List area. Type *.exe,

Displaying all files in a directory

and then press Enter to display only those files with an EXE extension. Your screen now looks like this:

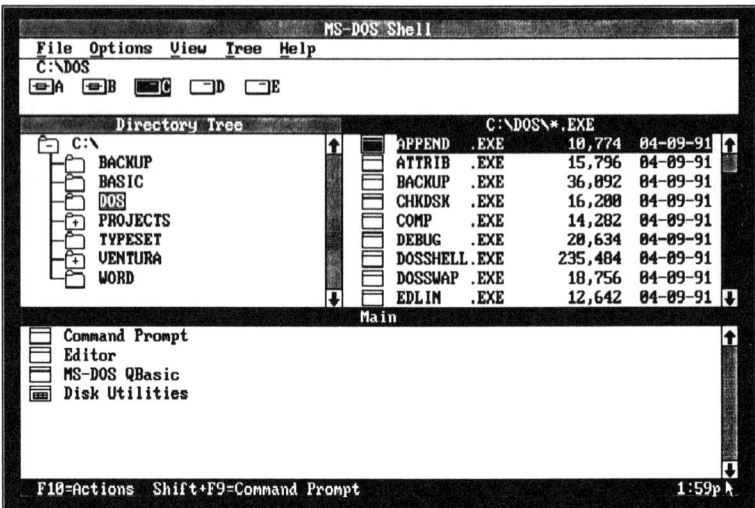

Next, display all the files in the DOS directory that have three or fewer letters in their filenames and any extension:

1. From the Options menu, choose File Display Options.
2. Type *???.** in the text box, and press Enter or click OK. The screen now looks like this:

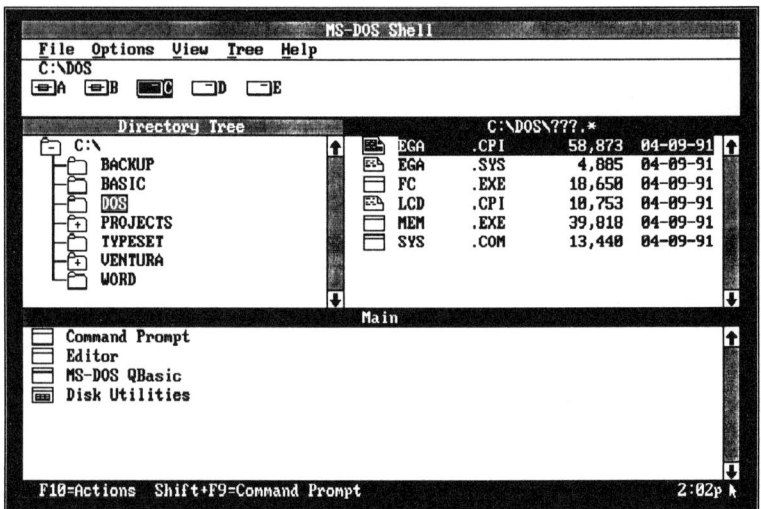

Selecting files in the Shell   While we are in the Shell, let's take a look at other methods of selecting files. First, display all the files in the DOS directory.

1. From the Options menu, choose File Display Options.
2. Type *.*, and then press Enter or click OK.

Now select the first four sequential files in the File List area
using the keyboard:

Selecting
sequential files

1. Tab to the File List area. The first file should be
   highlighted; press the Home key if it isn't.
2. Now hold down the Shift key and press the Down
   Arrow key three times. Your screen looks like this:

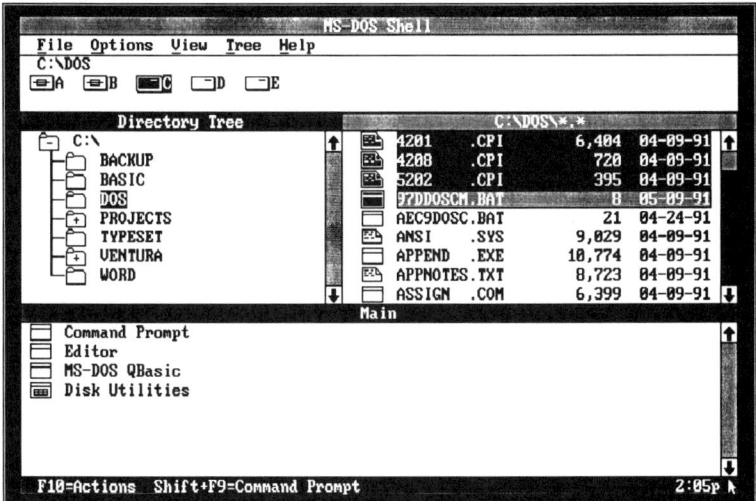

To do the same thing using the mouse follow these steps:

1. Press the Home key to reselect only the first file.
2. Hold down the Shift key and click the fourth file in the
   directory. Your screen looks as shown previously.

Selecting nonsequential files is a bit more involved. Let's
select the first, third, and fifth files in the directory, first using
the keyboard:

Selecting non-
sequential files

1. Press the Home key to reselect only the first file.
2. Press Shift-F8. Notice that the word *Add* appears in the
   status bar in the bottom right corner of the screen.
3. Press the Down Arrow key twice to skip over the
   second file (notice that it is not highlighted), and then
   press the Spacebar to select the third file.
4. Press the Down Arrow key two more times, and press
   the Spacebar to select the fifth file.
5. Press Shift-F8 to turn off Add mode.

That's it. Your screen now looks like the one on the next page.

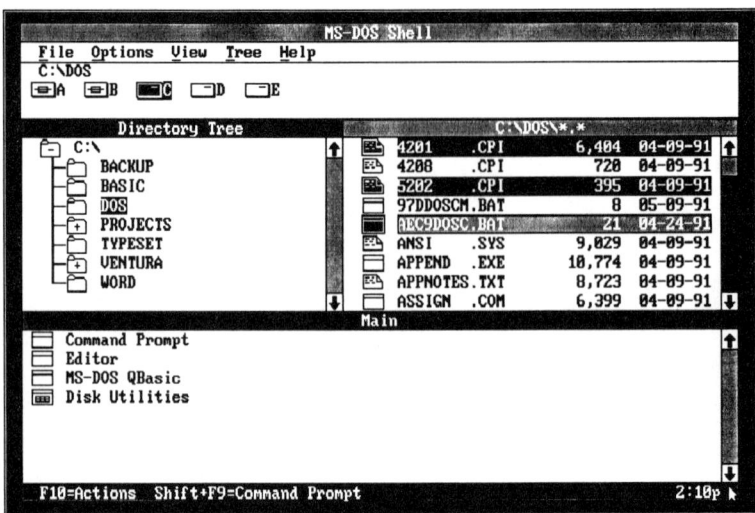

Now we'll do the same thing using the mouse

1. Press the Up Arrow key until only the first file is selected.

2. Hold down the Ctrl key, and click the third file.

3. Continue holding down the Ctrl key, and click the fifth file.

Selecting and deselecting all displayed files

The Shell also offers an easy way to select or deselect all the displayed files. Try this feature now:

1. From the File menu, choose Deselect All.

Only the last file you selected remains highlighted. As you would expect, Select All—located just ahead of Deselect All on the File menu—selects all the files displayed in the File List area.

Now that you know how to select files, let's take a look at what you can do with them.

Organizing Your Files

You organize your files by creating a logical hierarchy of drives and directories in which you can store your files for easy retrieval. You have seen how to set up the hierarchy. Now we'll take a look at how you copy and move files. The Shell and command-line methods for copying and moving files are very different. The Shell procedure is the onscreen equivalent of the physical process of shuffling pieces of paper from one file folder to another, whereas the command

line procedure is more abstract—you enter a command, and
DOS follows your orders behind the scenes. In the following
sections, we look at both procedures.

Copying Files

Copying files is usually a simple matter of creating a duplicate of a file in another directory. (You cannot create a copy
in the same directory without renaming the file; see page 51
for more information.) Sometimes, copying files to another
location on your hard drive makes sense. Perhaps you want
to store a copy of a file in an ARCHIVE directory while you
continue working on it in the current directory. But be
warned: Except for archiving purposes, creating multiple
copies of the same document on your hard drive can be
hazardous. It's easy to make changes in one version that
won't be reflected in the copies.

With that said, let's copy a few files, first from the Shell.
We're going to copy all the Basic files from the C:\DOS
directory into the BASIC directory that you created earlier.
Start by selecting the files you want to copy:

1. Be sure the DOS directory is selected in the Directory
   Tree area.
2. Select the File List area, and choose File Display
   Options from the Options menu. All the Basic files in
   the DOS directory have a BAS extension, so type *.bas*
   in the text box, and press Enter. The File List area now
   displays only the Basic files:

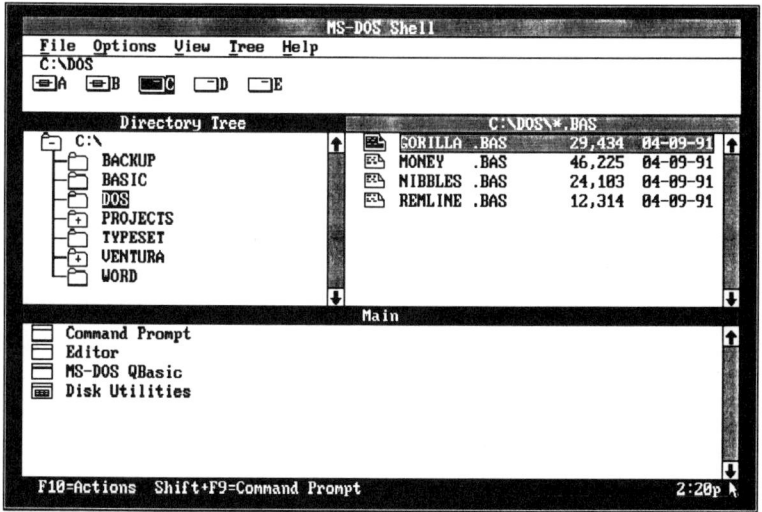

3. Having displayed all the files with a BAS extension, you can select them in one operation. Choose Select All from the File menu. DOS highlights all the files.

Now you're ready to copy the files.

Choosing the Copy command

1. Choose Copy from the File menu. The Copy File dialog box pops up:

Editing the list of files

2. The From box lists all on one line the names of the selected files, separated by spaces. You can use the Left Arrow key or the mouse to move through the list, and you can edit the filenames if you want. For now, simply type *c:\basic* in the To text box, to indicate the directory you want to copy the files to, and press Enter.

Copying with the mouse

In the Shell, you can copy files with the mouse simply by dragging the files to another directory or another drive. Position the mouse pointer over the selected file or files in the File List area, hold down the Ctrl key, press the mouse button, and drag the selected files to the desired directory or drive. In graphics mode, the mouse pointer changes into a file icon when you are over a directory or drive icon. Release the mouse button, and then release the Ctrl key. The Confirm Mouse Operation dialog box appears. If you are copying between directories, be sure the dialog box asks whether you want to *copy*, not *move*, the files. If all is well, click OK to copy the files. Otherwise, simply click No in the dialog box and try again. ♦

Copying and renaming

From the command line, you can copy and rename files in a single step. By modifying the **copy** command in the example on these pages, you can copy the files from the BASIC directory to the BACK-UP directory and change their extensions to BBK in one step. Here is the command that does the job:

copy *.* c:\backup*.bbk ♦

3. Check that the files are safely stowed in the BASIC directory by selecting it in the Directory Tree area. The Basic files are now displayed in the Files List area.

Now try using the **copy** command from the command line:

1. Press Shift-F9 to move to the command line. You should still be in the BASIC directory. If you haven't modified your command prompt (to do so, see page 43), check which directory you are in by entering *dir*. If you are not in the BASIC directory, enter *cd c:\basic* to switch to the BASIC directory.

2. Using the asterisk wildcard, copy all the files from the current directory (BASIC) to the BACKUP directory by typing *copy *.* c:\backup* and pressing Enter.

    Take a minute to analyze this command, and you'll see that you have just told DOS to copy (**copy**) all the files in the current directory (***.***) to the BACKUP directory (**c:\backup**).

Entering the copy command

3. Check DOS 's work by entering *dir \backup* to display a list of the Basic files in the BACKUP directory.

Renaming Files

During the course of your work, you will sometimes want to change a filename, perhaps to create groups of files with similar names, as suggested earlier in the chapter, or to differentiate between versions of the same file. For example, you might want to make it clear that the files in the BASIC directory are copies of the Basic files by changing their extensions from BAS to COP (for *copy*), and that the files in the BACKUP directory are backup copies by changing their extensions to BBK (for *Basic backup*).

Let's do that now. While we are still on the command line and in the BASIC directory, we'll use wildcard characters with the **ren** command to change all the BAS extensions to COP, like this:

1. Type *ren *.bas *.cop*, and press Enter.
2. Verify that everything went as planned by entering *dir* to display the renamed files.

Entering the ren command

Now let's rename a file from the Shell:

1. Type *exit*, and press Enter.

2. Select the BACKUP directory in the Directory Tree area.

3. You need to update the Shell screen to display the files you copied to this directory from the command line, so choose Refresh from the View menu. If necessary, reselect the BACKUP directory.

Choosing the Rename command →

4. Move to the File List area, where the first Basic file is highlighted, and choose Rename from the File menu.

5. DOS displays the Rename File dialog box and prompts you for a new name for the file:

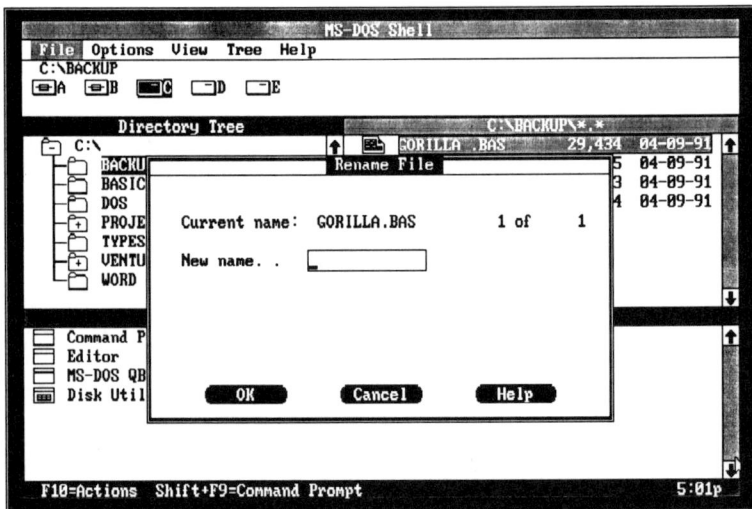

6. Type the name with a BBK extension, and press Enter. The new filename disappears from the list because only files with BAS extensions are currently displayed in the File List area.

7. From the Options menu, choose File Display Options, type *.*, and press Enter. You can now see the renamed file.

As you can imagine, renaming a group of files from the Shell can be tedious, because DOS displays a dialog box prompting you to enter a new name for each one. If you have more than one file to rename, it's faster to do it on the command line.

Deleting Files

If you followed along with the previous examples, you now have three sets of the same Basic files in three different directories on your hard disk. That's all well and good if you have storage space to spare, but for most of us, disk space is not something to waste. Moreover, a cluttered hard disk can decrease your computer's performance (see page 103 for more information). You can delete the extraneous files from the current directory (BACKUP) like this:

1. Press Shift-F9 to move to the command line.
2. Check that you are in the BACKUP directory. (If necessary, type *cd c:\backup* and press Enter to change directories.)
3. Now type *del *.** at the command prompt, and press Enter. ◄──── *Entering the del command*
4. DOS warns you that all the files in the directory will be deleted. Type *y* and press Enter to confirm that you want to delete the files.
5. Verify that the files are gone by entering *dir* at the command prompt. DOS displays the . and .. entries but no files. They are indeed gone.

Now let's delete the files from the BASIC directory using the Shell:

1. Type *exit* and press Enter to return to the Shell, and then select the BASIC directory.
2. Activate the File List area, and choose Select All from the File menu to select all the files.
3. Choose Delete from the File menu, or—even easier— press the Delete key. This dialog box appears: ◄──── *Choosing the Delete command*

```
╔════════════════════ MS-DOS Shell ════════════════════╗
 File  Options  View  Tree  Help
 C:\BASIC
 ▭A  ▭B  ▭C  ▭D  ▭E
 ┌──────── Directory Tree ────────┬──────── C:\BASIC\*.* ────────┐
 │ ┌─ C:\                      ↑ │ 📄 GORILLA .COP    29,434  04-09-91 ↑│
 │ ├─ BA┌──────────── Delete File ──────────────┐04-09-91 │
 │ ├─ BA│                                         │04-09-91 │
 │ ├─ DO│                                         │04-09-91 │
 │ ├─ PR│  Delete . .    Y.COP NIBBLES.COP REMLINE.COP │
 │ ├─ TY│                                         │
 │ ├─ UE│                                         │
 │ └─ WO│     ▐ OK ▌      ▐ Cancel ▌      ▐ Help ▌ │
 │       └─────────────────────────────────────────┘  ↓│
 ├──────────────────── Main ────────────────────┐
 │ ▭ Command Prompt                             ↑│
 │ ▤ Editor                                      │
 │ ▤ MS-DOS QBasic                               │
 │ ▣ Disk Utilities                              │
 │                                               ↓│
 F10=Actions  Shift+F9=Command Prompt              5:07p
╚═══════════════════════════════════════════════════════╝
```

4. Select the OK command button to indicate that you want to delete the selected files.

5. DOS then double-checks that you haven't selected any of the files by mistake, by displaying a confirmation dialog box for each file. Select Yes for all but two files. Save the last two by selecting No in their confirmation dialog boxes.

With two files remaining in the BASIC directory, we will move on to a discussion of moving files.

Moving Files

Moving files from within the Shell is a simple process. We'll practice by moving the remaining two files from the BASIC directory to the BACKUP directory.

1. Check that the two files in the BASIC directory are displayed in the File List area and are both selected.

Choosing the Move command

2. Choose Move from the File menu. This dialog box appears:

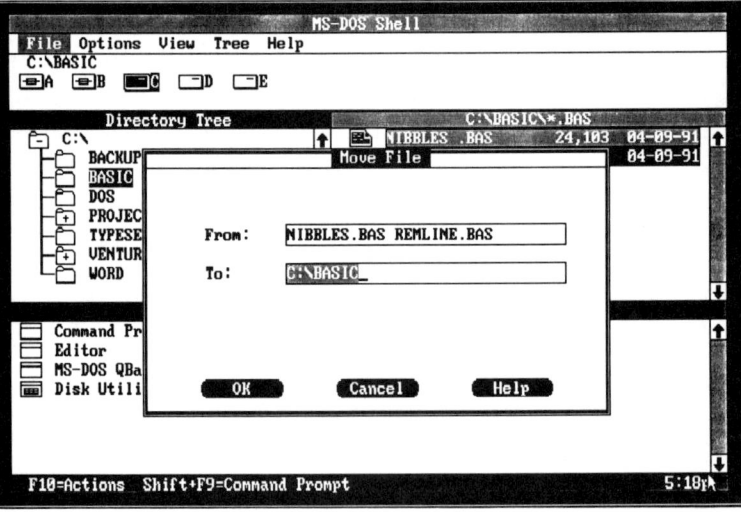

3. Type in the destination, *c:\backup*, and press Enter. DOS displays the message *No files in selected directory* in the File List area, because the directory is now empty.

4. Select the BACKUP directory to verify that the files have moved.

5. The File List area displays files in addition to the two we just moved. Why? Because we didn't refresh the

screen after we used the **del** command to delete the files from the BACKUP directory. Do that now, by choosing Refresh from the View menu and reselecting the BACKUP directory in the Directory Tree area. The File List area then displays the two COP files that you just moved from the BASIC directory.

You cannot move files in one step on the command line. You have to copy the files to their new location and then delete them from the old location. This is one procedure that is quicker and easier in the Shell.

Two-step moving

Deleting Directories

Let's tidy up a bit by deleting the BASIC and BACKUP directories, first from the Shell:

1. The directory you want to delete must be empty (no files or subdirectories), so delete the two files from the BACKUP directory by selecting both files and choosing the Delete command from the File menu. Confirm that you want to delete each file.

2. Now delete the BACKUP directory by checking that BACKUP is selected in the Directory Tree area and then simply pressing the Delete key. The Delete Directory Confirmation dialog box appears. Answer Yes to the prompt, and the directory is gone.

Deleting directories with the Delete key

Confirmation settings	But I needed that file!	Moving with the mouse
Choosing the Confirmation command from the Options menu displays the Confirmation dialog box. By default, DOS asks you to confirm file deletions and replacements and certain mouse actions. If you find the confirmation checks annoying, you can eliminate them by deselecting them. However, we do suggest leaving the Confirm on Delete check box selected. ♦	If you accidentally delete files you need, you might be able to recover them using the **undelete** command. It is very important to use the **undelete** command as soon as you realize you have made a mistake. See page 68 for instructions on how to use the **undelete** command. ♦	For those of you with a mouse, here is another way to move files. Select the files you want to move. Then drag the selection to the Directory Tree area, to the directory to which you want to move the files. (When the directory you want is highlighted, you are in the correct spot.) Release the mouse button, and answer the confirmation prompt. ♦

On the command line, you use the **rd** (Remove Directory) command to delete a directory, and you must be in a different directory when you enter the command. Follow these steps:

Entering the rd command

1. Press Shift-F9 to move to the command line, and check that you are in the root directory.
2. Type *rd \basic*, and press Enter.
3. Type *exit* and press Enter to return to the Shell.
4. Choose Refresh from the View menu to update the screen, and note the absence of the BASIC directory.

Well, with that bit of housekeeping taken care of, let's move on to new topics.

Copying Files to and from Floppy Disks

When you buy a new application program that doesn't come with an installation program, you will need to copy program files from floppy disks to your hard disk. If you are not hooked up to a network but work on more than one computer or share files with colleagues, you will need to copy files to floppy disks to transport them to another machine. You might also want to copy files to floppy disks to safeguard yourself against loss of data should anything go wrong with your machine. In this discussion, we focus on copying procedures primarily as a means of backing up files, but bear in mind that the techniques we discuss here apply any time you want to copy to or from floppy disks.

Backup Strategies

Part of any effort to organize your files should include systems for backing up your files. The first question technicians will ask when you bring your sick computer into the shop for repair is "When did you last back it up?" As you shift uncomfortably from foot to foot, they will roll their eyes knowingly and say, "That long ago, huh." Just imagine the satisfaction it would give you to be able to respond calmly, "Yesterday."

The term *backing up* simply means making a copy of your files that will be available in case you have problems with your computer. You can use floppy disks, various tape drives, removable hard drives, and other computers as the storage medium for backups. If you work in a large company, your company probably employs someone whose job is to back up all work on all computers. Smaller companies might designate one person to be responsible for backup chores or might make each person responsible for their own backups. For purposes of this discussion, we assume you are backing up your own files to floppy disks.

Backing up is like flossing your teeth or taking out the garbage—necessary, but not very exciting. It's easy to put it off. But we can't stress the point enough: Sooner or later, something will go wrong, and you will lose valuable data. Just as a bad dental checkup can induce people to start flossing, losing data can, overnight, instill the habit of backing up. Storing copies of data safely off your machine can reduce disasters to mere inconveniences and make recovering your work a matter of simply copying it from a floppy disk. Taking some time to evaluate your needs and develop a simple and effective backup strategy can really pay off when the inevitable data loss occurs.

Inconvenience vs. disaster

DOS provides three commands that effectively back up files: **copy**, **xcopy**, and **backup**. Which command you use depends primarily on the volume of data to be backed up.

- The simplest strategy for backing up small amounts of data is to use the **copy** command.
- If you need to back up an entire directory and any subdirectories it contains, you might want to use the **xcopy** command.
- If you get to the point where you are backing up more than one disk worth of data, or if you want to back up single files that are larger than one disk, you will probably want to use the **backup** command.

The first step in making backups is to insert a formatted floppy disk in the appropriate drive, so let's take a slight detour to discuss the formatting of floppy disks.

Formatting Floppy Disks

Formatting is the process by which DOS divides the disk into areas called *sectors* so that it can track the locations of files.

Sectors

Beware: Formatting destroys any information previously stored on the disk. We'll walk through the process for formatting a disk both in the Shell and on the command line. With two floppy disks in hand, follow these steps:

1. In the Shell, select the Program List area, then select the Disk Utilities group, and press Enter to display the contents of the group. With a mouse, you can simply double-click the Disk Utilities group to display its component programs.

Selecting Format from Disk Utilities

2. Select the Format command (not Quick Format), and press Enter. The Format dialog box appears with drive A selected as the default drive to format:

```
                                  MS-DOS Shell
      File   Options   View   Help
      C:\
      [=]A  [=]B  [■]C  [ ]D  [ ]E
     ┌─┐ C:\
     │ │  D┌──────────────── Format ────────────────────┐
     │ │  P│                                          │er.
     │ │  T│   Enter the drive to format.             │
     │ │  V│                                          │
     │ │  W│   Parameters  . . .  [a:]_____  │
     │    │                                          │
     │    │     (  OK  )     ( Cancel )     ( Help )   │
     │    └──────────────────┬──┬────────────────────┘
     ───────────────────────[↓]─────── Disk Utilities ──────
      [▦] Main
      [ ] Disk Copy
      [ ] Backup Fixed Disk
      [ ] Restore Fixed Disk
      [ ] Quick Format
      [■] Format
      [ ] Undelete
      F10=Actions   Shift+F9=Command Prompt                     5:33p
```

Formatting low-density disks

3. If you are formatting a low-density disk in a high-density drive, you need to include the /f switch in the Format command. Press the Right Arrow key to add the switch without deleting the a: parameter, and then type a space followed by /f:360 if you have 5.25-inch disks or /f:720 if you have 3.5-inch disks.

4. Press Enter or click OK to begin the formatting process.

5. DOS prompts you to insert a floppy disk in drive A. Insert the disk, and press Enter.

6. When DOS finishes formatting the disk, it asks for a volume label (the descriptive name that appears at the top of the listing of files displayed when you enter the **dir** command). If you think such a description

might be useful, type a label, and press Enter. Otherwise, skip this step by simply pressing Enter.

7. Next, DOS displays information about the storage capacity of the disk and the number of bad (unusable)
sectors, if any. It then asks whether you want to format
another disk. Press N, and then press Enter.

Now format the other disk from the command line:

1. Press Shift-F9, insert a different disk in drive A, and
type *format a:*. If you are formatting a low-density disk
in a high-density drive, type *format a: /f:360*. Pause for
a moment to be sure you included the a: parameter, and
then press Enter.

Entering the format command

2. Repeat steps 5 through 7 above to format the disk.

You are now ready to backup your files. Let's start with the
copy command.

Using copy

To demonstrate using **copy** to transfer files to floppy disks,
let's use the BAS files from the DOS directory again.

1. At the command prompt, type *copy c:\dos*.bas a:*,
and press Enter. This command tells DOS to copy all
the files with the BAS extension in the DOS directory
to drive A, using the same filenames.

Entering the copy command

2. Check that the files have been copied by typing *dir a:*
and pressing Enter. DOS lists the Basic files.

Quicker formatting

When you are formatting
brand new disks, add the /u
switch to the **format** command. This switch tells the
format command not to save
unformatting information,
thereby speeding the formatting process. Use the /u
switch only when you are
certain you won't want to unformat the disk, as is obvi-
ously the case with a new
disk. ♦

Bad sectors

Bad sectors are parts of a disk
that have been damaged or
are otherwise unusable. If
DOS finds bad sectors as it is
formatting a disk, it notes
their locations so that information is not written to those
areas. Hard disks commonly
have some bad sectors, but if
a floppy disk has bad sectors,
it is best not to use it. ♦

Can't tell low from high?

You can tell low-density
from high-density disks by
glancing at the hole in the
center. If the hole has a band
around it, the disk is usually
low density. If there is no
band, the disk is usually
high-density. ♦

Now copy the same files from the Shell:

1. Type *exit* and press Enter to return to the Shell, and then move to the DOS directory.
2. From the Options menu, choose File Display Options, type **.bas* in the text box, and press Enter. The File List area now displays the names of your Basic files.
3. Choose Select All from the File menu.

Choosing the Copy command

4. Choose Copy from the File menu, type *a:* in the To text box, and press Enter.
5. Because these files already exist on the floppy disk in drive A, DOS displays the Replace File Confirmation dialog box. This dialog box lists the size and date of last modification for both files and asks if you want to replace the file on the destination drive. In our case, the size and date are identical because the files haven't changed since we copied them using the command line. Answer Yes to overwrite each file on the disk in drive A.

Overwriting warning

The moral of this example is: Be careful when using the **copy** command from the command line, because DOS does not alert you before overwriting files. And be especially cautious when using wildcards with **copy**. When in doubt, copy from the Shell.

Put this disk on one side for now. You will use it again in Chapter 4.

Copying with a mouse

You can copy selected files to a floppy disk by selecting and dragging them to a drive in the drive area. When the pointer is over the correct drive, release the mouse button to start the copy, responding to the prompts as necessary. When copying to a different drive, you don't have to hold down the Ctrl key as you do when copying to a different directory. If you simply drag the files, DOS assumes you are copying them. To move the files instead, hold down the Alt key as you drag them. ♦

Copy shortcut

DOS treats the current directory as the default destination directory, so you need to specify only the source directory with the **copy** command. For example, to copy all the files from the disk in drive A to the current directory, C:\WORD\LETTERS, you can type

   copy a:*.*
to carry out the task. ♦

Using xcopy

The **xcopy** command copies directories and subdirectories (even empty subdirectories). For example, to copy all the Basic files from the DOS directory on drive C to the disk in drive A, you would enter *xcopy c:\dos*.bas a:dos*. DOS asks whether *DOS* specifies a filename or directory name on drive A. Press D for directory. DOS then creates a DOS directory on the disk in drive A and copies all the files with the BAS extension into that directory. For more information on the powerful **xcopy** command, see page 142.

Using backup

The **backup** command offers yet another way to back up your files to floppy disks. A couple of points about the **backup** command are worth noting:

- The **backup** command uses entire floppy disks, erasing anything previously stored on them.
- This command stores files in a unique format that is not directly accessible. You must use the **restore** command to restore the files to the directory from which you backed them up before you can use them.

You can use the **backup** command from the Shell or the command line, with virtually identical procedures. To practice backing up a directory, do the following:

1. Tell DOS you want to use the **backup** command:
   - From the Shell, display the Disk Utilities group in the Program List area, and then select Backup Fixed Disk. The Backup Fixed Disk dialog box appears.

     Selecting Backup from Disk Utilities

   - Or from the command line, type *backup* and a space, but do not press Enter yet.

     Entering the backup command

   From this point on, the Shell and command line procedures are identical. We will back up all the DOS directory files that have a BAS extension.

2. Type *c:\dos*.bas a:*, and press Enter.
3. When prompted, insert in drive A the second disk you formatted earlier.
4. DOS reminds you that the contents of the disk in drive A will be erased. Press any key to proceed. The BAS

files fit easily on one disk. If you were backing up data that occupied more than a single disk, DOS would prompt you to insert a new disk as necessary. (Number the disks to reflect the order in which you used them.)

5. Display the names of the files on drive A:
    •   From the Shell, select the icon for drive A to display the files in the File List area.
    •   Or from the command line, enter *dir a:*.

Instead of the Basic files, the list shows only two files: BACKUP.001, which contains the information from all the BAS files; and CONTROL.001, which contains information about the location of the files that enables the **restore** command to restore the files to their correct directories.

The **backup** command has several switches that allow it to back up files based on their dates and times and on whether they have changed since the last backup. You can also add files to a backup disk without erasing old backup files. See page 112 for more information.

Restoring Files

If Murphy's Law proves correct and you need to restore files from disk, keep these factors in mind:

•   The **restore** command restores files to the exact location from which they came. For example, files backed up from the C:\WORD\LETTERS directory are restored to that

Software backup options	Hardware backup options	Backup limitations
Because backing up files is such a universal chore, many software firms have tried to improve on the DOS **backup** command—some with considerable success. These programs typically offer faster backup and data compression, and are often menu-driven. You might want to investigate them if you perform frequent backups. ♦	In addition to software backup solutions, you might investigate backup hardware. Options in this area include removable hard drives, internal and external tape drives, Bernoulli boxes, and optical drives. Tape drives are on the lower end of the price scale and optical drives are on the upper end. ♦	If you are using **backup** in conjunction with a network, be aware that you can back up only those files to which you have access rights. On a related note, you should not use the **backup** command on a drive affected by the **join**, **assign**, or **subst** command. Refer to Chapter 6 for more information about these commands. ♦

directory. If you have removed this directory in the meantime, DOS recreates it when it restores the files.

- The **restore** command overwrites any files that have the same names as those it is restoring, and any changes you have made since you backed up the files are then lost. Move the files to another directory, or tell DOS to warn you before it overwrites a file, by using the /p switch when you enter the **restore** command. This applies to both the command line and the Shell.

To follow along with the next example, you need to simulate the accidental deletion of the Basic files from your DOS directory, by changing their extensions like this:

1. At the command prompt (press Shift-F9 if necessary), type *ren c:\dos*.bas c:\dos*.bbk*, and press Enter.

Now the BAS files are gone. Restore them from the backup disk you just created, by following these steps:

1. Tell DOS you want to use the **restore** command:
   - From the Shell, display the Disk Utilities group in the Program List area, and select Restore Fixed Disk. The Restore Fixed Disk dialog box appears.

     Selecting Restore from Disk Utilities

   - Or from the command line, type *restore* and a space, but do not press Enter yet.

     Entering the restore command

2. Type *a: c:* and press Enter. The first parameter, *a:*, is where DOS will find the files to restore, and the second parameter, *c:*, specifies where to restore the files.
3. DOS prompts you to insert the first backup disk in drive A. Insert the disk, and press any key.

If you were backing up data from more than a single disk, DOS would prompt you to insert the other disks as necessary.

From this simple demonstration, you can see how easily you can recover files in the event of a catastrophe—if you have taken precautions ahead of time. We discuss other ways of recovering data in Chapter 4.

A Sample Backup System

Many factors will influence the backup system you develop, including how often you update files and how much damage would result if you lost, say, a day's work. Following is an example of a pretty rigorous backup system.

- You set aside five disks, or groups of disks, labeled *Monday*, *Tuesday*, *Wednesday*, and so on. You also set aside a sixth disk, or group of disks, labeled *End of Week*.
- At the end of each day, you back up your files to that day's disk(s). For this daily procedure, you use the /d:*date* switch to back up only the files you have modified since yesterday, which speeds up the backup process. (See page 112 for more information.)
- At the end of each week, you back up all the files on your hard disk to the End of Week disk(s).
- The cycle starts over at the beginning of the next week.

You can modify this backup system in many ways to meet your individual needs. For example, if you have copies of the original disks for all the software on your machine, you will probably choose not to back up those files at the end of each week. Or you might add a seventh set of disks for keeping a backup of the entire contents of your hard disk away from your office to safeguard your data against fire or vandalism. You might also want to simplify the backup process by using batch files. (See page 86 for more information about batch files.)

Organizing Programs

So far we have talked about ways you can organize your data files. In this last section, we look at some ways to set up programs so that you can work efficiently.

Using Groups

The DOS Shell provides a mechanism, called *groups*, for organizing program files in the Program List area. Although creating and manipulating groups is beyond the scope of this book, we'll briefly explain the concept here.

Groups provide a way to arrange the names of programs so that they are visible at the same time in the Program List area, even though they may be stored in different directories on your hard drive. For example, here at Online Press we have created a group called *Publish*. In this group is a word-processing program, a graphics program, a grammar-checking program, and a desktop-publishing program. In one convenient place, we can access all the tools we need for working with manuscripts. If your work demands that you use a variety of programs, you might want to explore the topic of groups in the DOS documentation.

Associating Extensions with Programs

If you use data files that have certain extensions with specific programs, you can make loading the files into the program a one-step process, by associating the extension with the program. For example, if you use data files with the extension RPT with your word processor, you can associate RPT with the word processor so that simply selecting the data file loads it and the word processor. To make this association:

1. In the Shell, move to the directory that contains the word-processing program, and select the program file.
2. Choose Associate from the File menu. The Associate File dialog box pops up.
3. Type the extension you want to associate (without the period) in the Extensions box; for example, type *rpt*. To associate more than one extension with the same program, type them all, separating them with spaces. Then press Enter.

Now you can simply select a data file with that extension in the File List area and press Enter, or double-click it with the mouse, to load the file into its associated program.

Switching Between Programs

A powerful feature of the DOS Shell is the Task Swapper, which allows you to keep several programs open at one time and switch between them, without having to quit one program and load another. For example, if you are working on a document in your word processor and you need to check figures from a spreadsheet, you don't have to quit the word processor to open the spreadsheet.

Starting the Task Swapper is as simple as choosing Enable Task Swapper from the Options menu. If you start the Task Swapper after choosing Program List or Program/File Lists from the View menu, the Active Task List area appears in the bottom-right corner of the screen.

Starting Task Swapper

After enabling Task Swapper, you can start a program by choosing Run from the File menu and typing the program name, or by choosing the program file from either the File List or Program List area. To leave that program without quitting and return to the Shell, press Ctrl-Esc. DOS displays the name of the program you have started in the Active Task List area. You can then start another program. For example, you might start a word processor, such as Microsoft Word, type a memo, switch to the Shell by pressing Ctrl-Esc, and then start a spreadsheet program, such as Lotus 1-2-3. If you press Ctrl-Esc to quit Lotus and return to the Shell, you see both Word and Lotus listed in the Active Task List area.

Active Task List area

To move from one open program to another, hold down the Alt key and press the Tab key. You can cycle through the list of open programs by holding down Alt and repeatedly pressing Tab.

Before you can quit Task Swapper, leave the Shell, or turn off your computer, you must quit each active program from within that program. As you quit each one, its name disappears from the Active Task List area. When the Active Task List area is empty, you can safely quit Task Swapper by choosing Disable Task Swapper from the Options menu, leave the Shell, or turn off your machine.

Quitting Task Swapper

In this long chapter, we have tried to cover as many bases as possible, giving you an overview of the tools DOS offers to help you get organized. Now it's up to you!

4

When Things Go Wrong

The title of this chapter is "When Things Go Wrong" not "If Things Go Wrong." For good reason. Sooner or later you'll accidentally delete an important file, or an application program will crash and corrupt some of your data, or you will format the wrong disk, or DOS will display a message you don't understand and you'll be stuck, not knowing what to do. Depending on how well-prepared you are for such an event, it could be a minor inconvenience or a major catastrophe.

In this chapter, we start with problems you might encounter with individual files, then we move on to problems with disks and programs. We show you how to avoid some problems and how to minimize the impact of others. We also translate some common DOS error messages and give you pointers about how to respond to them.

Because reading this chapter might be prompted by an emergency, we start with immediate guidance about how to recover deleted files and unformat disks.

You've Deleted the Wrong File

Recovering a deleted file can be a straightforward process as long as you catch your mistake before you save, move, or copy another file to the disk where the deleted file was stored. You recover individual files with a new DOS 5 command called **undelete**. (Note that the **undelete** command doesn't work on a networked drive.)

Let's give the **undelete** command a try with copies of the Basic files. If you've turned to this section in a moment of desperation, start with step 3, working in the directory from which you deleted your file or files.

1. Create a C:\BASIC directory, and copy into it the files with the BAS extension from the DOS directory, just as you did in Chapter 3. (If necessary, follow the steps on page 49.)

2. Move to the C:\BASIC directory, and delete the BAS files. Oops! That's not what you meant to do.

3. With the BASIC directory still selected, run the **un-delete** command:
   - From the Shell, select Undelete from the Disk Utilities group in the Program List area, and press Enter. The Undelete dialog box appears:

Selecting Undelete from Disk Utilities

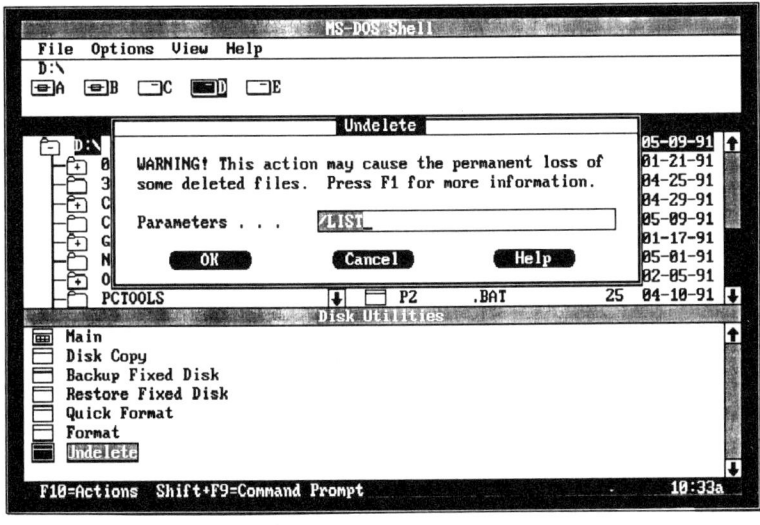

   - Or from the command line, type *undelete /list*.
4. The /list parameter instructs DOS to list the deleted files and tell you whether they are recoverable; it does not actually undelete the files. Press Enter to display the list of deleted files.

Entering the undelete command

5. To undelete the files:
   - From the Shell, again choose Undelete from the Disk Utilities group in the Program List area, and press Enter. When DOS displays the Undelete dialog box, press the Backspace key to delete the /LIST parameter, and then press Enter or click OK.
   - Or from the command line, simply type *undelete*, and press Enter.
6. DOS displays the name of a deleted file, with a question mark as the first letter in the filename, and asks whether you want to recover the file. Press Y for *yes*, and then type the first letter of the filename. (If you can't remember the first letter, any letter will do. You can change it later.)

7. DOS lets you know that the file was successfully undeleted and then displays the name of the next deleted file. Repeat the previous step for each file that you want to recover.

As you can see, using the **undelete** command isn't difficult, and if you realize right away that you've made a mistake, the command is very reliable. If you don't realize you've made a mistake until later, you might have to rely on backup files to restore the deleted information. See page 56 for more information about backing up files.

You've Formatted the Wrong Disk

Unformatting limitations

With version 5, DOS has a new **unformat** command that enables you to restore entire disks that have been accidentally reformatted. The catch is that, for the most reliable results, the formatting operation you want to undo must have been carried out using the DOS 5 **format** command, and you must not have used the /u switch, which formats disks without recording any information necessary for unformatting.

How can DOS unformat disks? When you use the DOS 5 **format** command, DOS saves old format information before

---

Understanding Undelete	**A missed recovery**	**Unformat immediately**
When DOS deletes a file, it doesn't destroy the data in the file. It simply marks the space allocated to the file as available for other data. The deleted file remains on your hard disk until it is overwritten by another file. This is why it is important to avoid writing data to the hard disk and to use the **undelete** command immediately after accidentally deleting a file. ♦	If, as you are working through a list of files to undelete, you accidentally answer *no* for a file you want to recover, don't worry. Continue working through the remaining files, and then run the **undelete** command again to recover the file you missed the first time. ♦	You should run the **unformat** command before copying any files to the disk you want to unformat. As with **undelete**, the sooner you discover your mistake the better. ♦

formatting the disk. The **format** commands of earlier versions of DOS didn't save this information. Although the **unformat** command is sometimes able to recover data from a disk without the old format information, recovery under these circumstances is much less reliable. Recovery is also unreliable if you store information on the newly formatted disk before using the **unformat** command.

Unformatting a disk is a fairly simple process, but you might want to practice the steps ahead of time. Then you'll know what to do in an emergency. If you are in the midst of an emergency now, skip the first part of this example and follow the steps for unformatting on the next page, substituting your disk information where appropriate. Otherwise, using the floppy disk to which you copied the Basic files in Chapter 3, first format the disk:

1. Insert the disk in drive A, and format it as follows:
    *   From the Shell, choose Format from the Disk Utilities group in the Program List area. The Format dialog box indicates that, by default, DOS will format drive A, so simply press Enter.

        Formatting from the Shell

    *   From the command line, type *format a:*.

        Formatting from the command line

        (Remember, to format a low-density disk in a high-density drive, you must use the /f:360 switch. See page 57 for more information.)
2. Press Enter in response to the *Insert new diskette* message. DOS tells you it is saving unformatting information and then formats the disk. When DOS finishes, it prompts you to supply a volume label. For this example, press Enter to specify no volume label, and then press N for *no* to decline DOS's offer to format another disk.
3. Now check the disk in drive A, either by selecting drive A in the Shell's drive area or by typing *dir a:* on the command line. The disk is blank.

If this scenario were real, you would start to break out in a cold sweat as you realized you had formatted the wrong disk, only to breath a sigh of relief as you remembered the **unformat** command. To unformat the disk, follow these steps:

1. You have to run **unformat** from the command line, so if you are working in the Shell, press Shift-F9 to display the command line.

2. Type *unformat a:*, and press Enter. When prompted, insert the disk and press Enter. DOS then displays this warning message:

Entering the unformat command

```
C:\>unformat a:

Insert disk to rebuild in drive A:
and press ENTER when ready.


Restores the system area of your disk by using the image file created
by the MIRROR command.

     WARNING !!        WARNING !!

This command should be used only to recover from the inadvertent use of
the FORMAT command or the RECOVER command.  Any other use of the UNFORMAT
command may cause you to lose data!  Files modified since the MIRROR image
file was created may be lost.

Searching disk for MIRROR image.

The last time the MIRROR or FORMAT command was used was at 11:02 on 05-10-91.

The MIRROR image file has been validated.

Are you sure you want to update the system area of your drive A (Y/N)?
```

3. Press Y to update the system area (the area where information about file locations is stored), thereby unformatting the disk. DOS then reports that the unformat operation was successful.

Running the Mirror command

Notice the reference to the **mirror** command in the message DOS displays before it unformats the disk. The **mirror** command stores information about a disk so that if the disk is inadvertently formatted, the **unformat** command can reconstruct the disk.

DOS saves the unformatting information in two files. MIRORSAV.FIL is a hidden, read-only file; MIRROR.FIL is a read-only file. You only need to be aware of them so that you do not delete them.

To be effective, the **mirror** command should be run frequently. We suggest that you add the **mirror** command on a line by itself in your AUTOEXEC.BAT file, so that the command runs each time you start your system. The following command saves information from drive C:

   mirror c:

See page 29 for information about how to add commands such as this one to your AUTOEXEC.BAT file. ♦

4. Now check the disk in drive A by typing *dir a:* and pressing Enter. DOS lists the files stored on the disk.

That's all there is to unformatting a disk under ideal conditions. If conditions are less than ideal—for example, if data has been written to the newly formatted disk or the disk was formatted with a version of DOS earlier than 5—you can expect to lose data during the unformatting operation. Even with these drawbacks, it's great to know that formatting is no longer a completely irreversible process.

Your Application Programs Don't Work Well with DOS 5

Some application programs are designed to work with specific versions of DOS, such as DOS 3. When you load these programs, they check which version of DOS your computer is running and quit if they find an unexpected version number, even though they may work perfectly well with DOS 5.

To get around this problem, DOS 5 comes with a program called Setver that is automatically loaded when you turn on your computer. (The instruction to load Setver is put into your CONFIG.SYS file when you install DOS 5.) Setver indicates the version of DOS that is to be reported to certain programs, effectively tricking those programs into thinking that they are running under the version of DOS they were designed to work with.

Tricking programs designed for an earlier version

If you have trouble running a program that worked perfectly well with an earlier version of DOS, you should verify that the program is otherwise compatible with DOS 5 by contacting the program's manufacturer. If the program is compatible, you can add the program and an earlier DOS version number to the Setver list by using the **setver** command. Here's how:

1. On the command line, type *setver*, followed by a space, the program filename, and the DOS version number for which the program was designed. Then press Enter.

Entering the setver command

Here's an example of a hypothetical use of **setver**:

setver yourprog.exe 3.3

What if the manufacturer says the program is not compatible with DOS 5? Then you have to decide between DOS 5 and the program you want to run. If the program's importance to your work outweighs the advantages of using DOS 5, you need to switch to an earlier version of DOS to maintain compatibility. If you upgraded to DOS 5 from an earlier version of DOS, returning to your old version of DOS is a simple matter of using the Uninstall disk(s) created during the DOS 5 installation process. If you did not install DOS 5 and you have no Uninstall disk(s), you will have to find an earlier version of DOS and install it following the instructions in its manual.

To return to your previous version of DOS from DOS 5:

Uninstalling DOS 5

1. Insert the disk labeled *Uninstall1* in drive A, and reboot your system.
2. When the Uninstall program appears on your screen, follow its instructions to install your previous version of DOS.

If you later decide you want to work in DOS 5, you will have to reinstall it from scratch, using the installation program.

Common Error Messages

When something goes wrong, DOS displays a message to indicate the nature of the problem. If you don't speak the same language as DOS, however, these error messages may not help much. In this section, we spotlight a few of the most common error messages. In each case, we try to give you ideas about what might be causing the message, how serious it is, and how you might fix the problem.

Access denied DOS displays this message if you try to delete or save a write-protected, read-only, or locked file. To access a write-protected floppy disk, remove the tape from the write-protection notch on the disk, To access a read-only file, use the **attrib** command to remove the read-only attribute (see page 111). In the Shell, DOS allows you to delete read-only files after asking for confirmation. If a file is locked, someone else on your network is using the file. You will have to wait until that person is finished with the file.

Bad command or filename   DOS can't find a command, program, or file with the name you typed. Aside from a simple misspelling, the most likely cause of this problem is that the item in question is stored in a directory that is not in the current path. Switch to the directory in which the file is stored, and reenter the command, program, or filename, or modify the **path** command in your AUTOEXEC.BAT file to include the directory that contains the command, program, or file. (See page 31 for more information about the **path** command and the AUTOEXEC.BAT file.)

Bad or missing Command Interpreter   This message means that the COMMAND.COM file has become corrupted or has been moved or deleted from the root directory. If you create a bootable disk, you can copy the COMMAND.COM file from that disk to the root directory of drive C. Here's how to create a bootable disk:

1. Insert a blank, formatted floppy disk in drive A.
2. On the command line, type *sys a:*, and press Enter. DOS then copies the three files to the disk in drive A.
3. It's a good idea to include your AUTOEXEC.BAT and CONFIG.SYS files on this disk, but you don't want DOS to process these files if you have to use the bootable disk, because they might reference locations on the hard disk that are not currently accessible. To prevent DOS from processing the files, create a directory called FILES on the disk, and copy your AUTOEXEC.BAT and CONFIG.SYS files to that directory.
4. Stow the disk away in a safe place as insurance.

Creating a bootable disk

Now if COMMAND.COM gets deleted or corrupted, you can use the bootable disk to boot your computer and replace this critical file.

Bad or missing *filename*   A device is incorrectly identified in your CONFIG.SYS file. Load CONFIG.SYS into the DOS Editor (see page 29), and check the spelling of the device name and the file's path.

Cannot *command* a network drive   If you are working on a network, you won't be able to use many DOS commands. On some networks, you might be able to unload the network software and proceed with the command, but don't try this solution unless you are absolutely sure you know what you are doing.

Duplicate filename or file not found   You might see this message when renaming a file, because the **ren** command will not overwrite an existing file. For example, if you try to rename ACCOUNTS.DOC as ACCOUNTS.BAK and you already have a file named ACCOUNTS.BAK in the directory, DOS displays this message.

General failure reading (or writing) drive *x*   This catch-all message indicates a drive problem, but DOS doesn't know exactly what it is. The cause might be some simple error on your part, such as inserting an unformatted disk in drive A or inserting a high-density disk in a low-density drive. Snoop around before you panic.

Name of list device[PRN]   DOS displays this message, if you use the **print** command for the first time without using the /d switch to specify an output device. DOS is asking where to send the output. If your printer is connected to the first parallel port (LPT1), you can respond by pressing Enter, because PRN defaults to LPT1. Otherwise, specify the serial or parallel port to which you want the output to go.

Out of environment space   This message may appear when the **set** command is run (either from a batch file or on the command line). You can increase the size of your environment by using the **shell** command. See the documentation for more information.

Program too big to fit in memory   You don't have enough memory to load the program you specified. Application programs usually indicate in their documentation how much memory must be available to run them. Run the **mem** command, and compare that memory requirement with the *largest executable program size* amount specified by **mem**. If you are short of memory, unload any programs you are running (for example, the Task Swapper), and try again.

Unrecognized command in CONFIG.SYS   A command is incorrectly specified in your CONFIG.SYS file. Load CONFIG.SYS into the DOS Editor (see page 29), and check that

all device names are correctly spelled and that the location
of each device is correctly indicated by its path.

Planning Ahead

So far in this chapter, we have focused on what to do when
things go wrong. Now let's take a look at a few things you
can do to avoid problems in the first place.

Safeguarding Your Files

An effective plan for safeguarding your files has two phases:
First, and most obvious, take steps to avoid losing them, and
second, back them up regularly so that they are easy to
recover if you do make a mistake.

    If you keep the following pointers in mind, you may never
have to deal with lost files:

- In the Shell, DOS displays confirmation dialog boxes
  when it wants you to think twice about a particular
  action. If you find the display of these dialog boxes too
  annoying, you can turn them off by using the Confirmation command on the Options menu, but you should
  leave as many of these safeguards as possible turned on.

  Confirmation boxes

- If you work on the command line, consider using the /p
  switch with the **del**, **replace**, **restore**, and **xcopy** commands. DOS then prompts you to confirm that you want
  to perform the corresponding action and thereby gives
  you an opportunity to change your mind.

- Keep files and directories organized (see Chapter 3). As
  a general rule, don't keep several copies of the same file
  in several different directories. If you work on one
  version of a file one day and on another version another
  day, you'll lose one set of changes. No program we
  know of can help you merge the changes so that they
  are all in one file.

  Keeping organized

    Following these tips will certainly keep the chances of
losing data to a minimum. But to reduce the impact of the
rare mishap, nothing works as well as backing up your files.
Backing up is a necessary chore, and one episode of lost data
is usually enough to convince people of the necessity for
solid backup procedures. These procedures can range from

A reminder: Back up your files

using the **copy** command to copy files to a floppy disk, to daily and weekly use of the **backup** command, to company-wide backups with commercial hardware and software systems. The important thing is to be able to restore your files in the event of an accident. (See page 56 for more information about backing up files.)

Maintaining Your Hard Disk

If you need to use DOS commands to recover lost files, the likelihood of successful recovery is greater if you regularly maintain your hard disk. In this context, maintenance entails routinely defragmenting the disk and checking the integrity of the file allocation table (FAT), which records the locations of all files on the disk. We'll briefly cover both maintenance procedures here.

Defragmenting your hard disk   The DOS package does not include a disk-defragmentation program. You can buy a disk-defragmentation program as part of a utility package such as Norton Utilities, PC Tools Deluxe, or Mace Utilities. A disk-defragmentation program makes files easier to un-delete and speeds up the operation of your machine by ensuring that each file is stored in one block of space on your hard disk.

How DOS stores files

Disk-defragmentation programs exist because of the way DOS stores files. Contrary to what you might expect, the information in a file is not necessarily stored contiguously but may be scattered throughout your hard disk. Your hard disk is divided into units called *clusters*, each with its own cluster number. As you work on a file—adding information here, deleting information there, and saving as you go—DOS stores the changes to the file in the first available cluster and uses the file allocation table (FAT) as a sort of address book to keep track of the clusters in which the parts of the file are located. Because fragments of the file can be stored in many places on the hard disk, the file can have many entries in the FAT. The file's first entry, known as the *directory entry*, tells DOS which entry in the FAT indicates the cluster that contains the beginning of the file. The file is then "chained" together, with each entry in the FAT containing the number of the cluster that has the next file fragment.

File allocation table

As a result, your hard drive can be a checkerboard of full and empty clusters. Disk-defragmentation programs use the FAT to find all the scattered parts of each file and store them together in a contiguous group of clusters. Undeleting a file is then easier, because the file is stored in one place. And when you work with files in an application program, DOS can open files faster, because it doesn't have to jump all over your hard drive to put the file together.

Checking the integrity of the FAT   You use the **chkdsk** command to check the FAT and display the results. If you use **chkdsk** without any switches, it gives general disk statistics. If you use **chkdsk** with a filename parameter, such as *.*, it alerts you when it finds any of the following:

- Data on the disk that doesn't have an entry in the FAT, a condition known as *lost clusters*.
- Two files that have been assigned to the same cluster, a condition known as *cross-linked files*.
- A noncontiguous, or fragmented, file.

If you use **chkdsk** with the /f switch, **chkdsk** repairs the problems it finds to the extent that it can. The safest course of action is to run **chkdsk** without the switch first to see what problems the program finds. Then proceed as follows:

- If **chkdsk** finds lost clusters, run the program again with the /f switch. When asked whether you want the clusters saved as files, answer *yes*. Each cluster is then saved in the root directory with a CHK extension. If **chkdsk** consistently finds lost clusters, you should examine the CHK files for possible clues about software misbehavior. Use the **type** command to display the file on the screen (see page 139 for more information). Usually, these files are unusable file fragments that you can simply delete. If you can tell that all the CHK files are from one program, check that the program is properly installed (or reinstall it).

  Lost clusters

- If **chkdsk** reports cross-linked files, don't run **chkdsk** with the /f switch if you have installed a utility package such as Norton Utilities, PC Tools Deluxe, or Mace Utilities. These packages include disk-repair tools that can correct this problem without loss of data, whereas

  Cross-linked files

using **chkdsk** will almost certainly result in loss of data from one of the cross-linked files. If you don't have one of these utility packages, go ahead and use **chkdsk** with the /f switch, and then replace the file that has lost data with the equivalent backup file.

As you've probably gathered, for all the improvements in DOS 5, we still feel that a utility package is a good investment. These packages cost about as much as one trip to the computer repair shop and may well pay for themselves many times over.

Preventing Power Problems

Deleting files and formatting disks isn't the only way to lose data. Unfortunately, power outages and power surges can make files or parts of files inaccessible not only by destroying unsaved information in memory but also by corrupting the FAT. You can buy accessories that provide various degrees of protection from the power problems that can result in corrupted disks, including the following:

- Surge protectors are power filters that detect and dissipate excess power. You plug the surge protector into an electrical outlet and then plug your computer into the surge protector. In many office buildings, surge protection is built into the power supply, and you may already have this level of protection for your computer.
- Voltage regulators combine power filtering and regulating to provide continuous voltage even in brownout conditions.
- If your work is critical, you might want to purchase a stand-by power supply to ensure uninterrupted power during power outages.

At one end of the spectrum, surge-protector prices start at about $10; at the other end, uninterruptible power supplies can cost thousands of dollars. Let the importance of your data and the frequency of power disturbances in your area guide your choice of protection accessories.

One last word of advice. The most important way of safeguarding your data is the easiest: Save your work often.

5

Enhancing Your Productivity

In previous chapters, you learned how to use DOS to manage files and troubleshoot problems. Now it's time to take that basic knowledge and turbocharge it with some of DOS's power features. In this chapter, we first introduce techniques for redirecting information from one command to another, and we briefly cover DOS's "filter" commands (**more**, **sort**, and **find**). Then you will be ready to delve into batch files, which can be significant labor- and time-savers. With batch files, you can run commands without having to remember the exact sequence of parameters and switches, and you can carry out lengthy processes, such as huge printing jobs, at night or during lunch. (Your computer works away while you are taking a break.) Also in this chapter, we take a look at the Doskey program, which allows you to run a command or series of commands simply by pressing a key or key combination.

Redirection: Changing Tracks

Like a switch on a railroad track, redirection allows you to divert information from its normal course to a different one. In this section, we explain how redirection works and show you ways you might want to use this powerful feature.

Redirection allows DOS to take input from a specified source or send output to a specified destination. DOS has four redirection symbols:

Redirection symbols

- One right angle bracket (>) directs the output of a command to a file or device. For example, entering *dir > dir.doc* creates a text file called DIR.DOC and stores the directory listing generated by the **dir** command in the file, instead of displaying the listing.
- Two right angle brackets (>>) direct the output of a command to a file without destroying the current contents of the file. In effect, the output is appended to the end of the file.
- One left angle bracket (<) directs the input from a file (or a filter—see page 85) to a command. For example, if you create DIR.DOC by entering the example command above, entering *more < dir.doc* sends the information in DIR.DOC to the **more** command, which then displays the information a screenful at a time.

- The pipe symbol (|) directs the input from a command to a filter (see page 85).

Redirecting the output of a command to a file is, perhaps, the most common form of redirection, because the output is then available for later viewing or manipulation. Try this:

Redirecting to a file

1. Type *dir c:\dos > dos.dir*, and press Enter. DOS creates a file called DOS.DIR and stores in it the output of the **dir** command (a list of the files in the C:\DOS directory).

2. Type *type dos.dir*, and press Enter. The contents of DOS.DIR scroll across your screen, probably too fast for you to see the first files in the list.

3. Type *more < dos.dir*, and press Enter. The **more** command displays one screenful of information and then stops, waiting for you to press a key to indicate that you are ready to see the next screenful. Press Ctrl-C when you've seen enough.

When redirecting output to an existing file, be careful to use two right angle brackets when you want to append the new information to the file. Using only one right angle bracket replaces the old information with the new. Experiment by using first one and then two right angle brackets:

Adding information to a file

1. Type *mem > dos.dir*, and press Enter.

2. Now take a look at DOS.DIR:
   - From the Shell, choose View File Contents from the File menu to look at the DOS.DIR file.

Device redirection

You can redirect information to devices as well as to files. Redirecting information to a printer is probably the most common example. To print a graphic representation of your directory structure, for example, redirect the output of the **tree** command to the printer, like this:

   tree > lpt1 ♦

Application redirection

Many application programs send output to your screen. By redirecting this output to a file, you can save this information for future reference. This redirection technique is especially handy if you are running programs from a batch file. We discuss batch files on page 86. ♦

It still goes to the screen?

Some application programs don't allow their output to be redirected. If you have tried to redirect the output of a program but the output still goes to the screen, there is nothing, short of asking the program's developer to change the application, that you can do about it. ♦

- Or from the command line, type *type dos.dir* and press Enter to display the contents of the file.

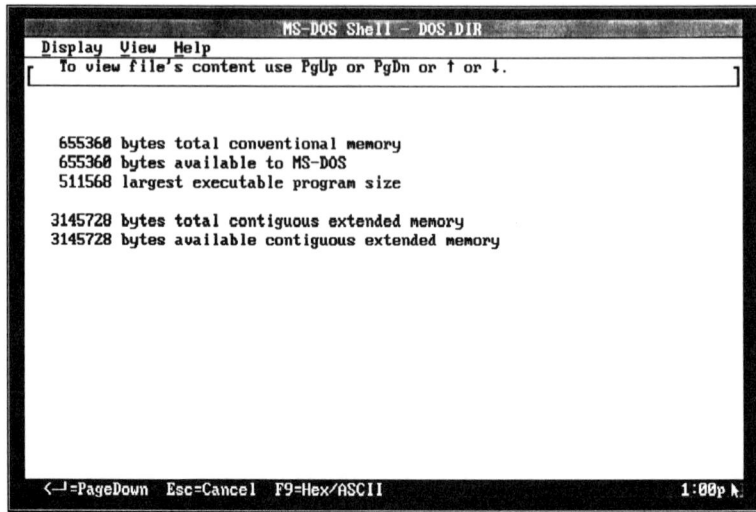

As you can see, the previous contents of DOS.DIR have been replaced with the **mem** command's report on your computer's memory.

3. Now enter *dir c:\dos >> dos.dir*, and again view the result. This time, DOS.DIR contains the output from **mem** followed by the output from **dir**.

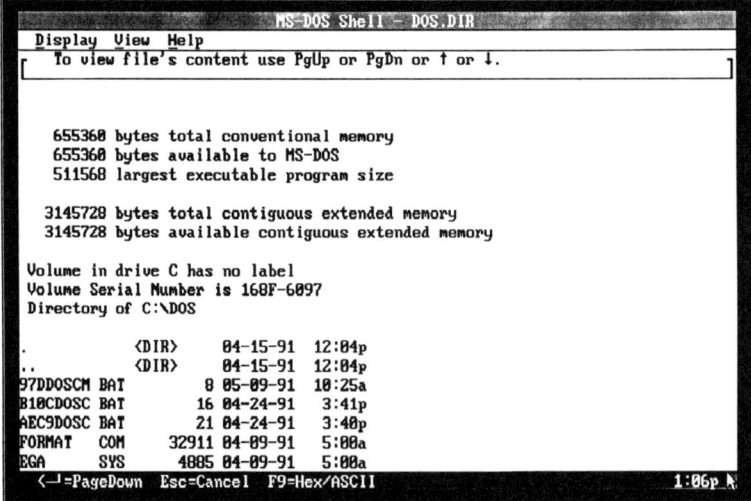

Filters

Filters are commands that work with streams of characters (most often files). DOS has three filter commands:

- The **more** command, as you have seen, takes information from a file or the output of another command and displays it one screenful at a time.
- The **sort** command takes information from a file or the output of another command and sorts it alphabetically, line by line.
- The **find** command takes information from a file or the output of another command and searches for the characters you specify, displaying the lines in which the characters occur, the lines in which the characters don't occur, or the number of times the characters occur, depending on which switches you use.

You use different symbols to direct information to filter commands depending on whether the information is coming from a file or from a command. Earlier, you used the left angle bracket (<) to direct information from the DOS.DIR file to the **more** command, as in

more < dos.dir

To direct the output of a command (or another filter) to a filter, you use a pipe symbol (|), as in

dir c:\dos | more

Here, the output of the **dir** command—a listing of the files in the DOS directory—serves as input to the **more** command.

You can use more than one redirection symbol on the command line. For example, to store an alphabetically sorted listing of the files in the C:\DOS directory in DOS.DIR, enter

Multiple redirection symbols

dir c:\dos | sort > dos.dir

Do you want DOS to sort the contents of a file and display the result one screenful at a time? Enter

sort < c:\dos\dosshell.ini | more

(Press Ctrl-C to interrupt this command when you have seen enough.)

Interrupting a command

Redirection and filters are powerful and flexible tools, and you'll soon find ways to make creative use of them.

Batch Files

Batch files save time, prevent errors, and add flexibility to your work with DOS. Almost anyone can make their computing life easier by using batch files.

A batch file is simply a DOS command or a collection of commands that you store in a text file that has a BAT extension. Entering the name of the batch file causes DOS to execute the commands contained in the file as if you had typed them on the command line. Sound simple? It is. But for some reason many people find batch files so intimidating that they never get around to investigating how to create and use them. This section will take the mystery out of batch files with a few down-to-earth examples.

Batch Files That Save Keystrokes

On the simplest level, you can use batch files to shorten command names. For example, if you find yourself loading and unloading the DOS Shell during the day, you can make life easier for yourself by creating a batch file to do the loading for you. Let's use the DOS Editor to create this batch file. In Chapter 2, you loaded the DOS Editor from the Shell. Here, we'll load the Editor from the command line, instead:

Entering the edit command

1. Move to the root directory, type *edit ds.bat*, and press Enter to load the DOS Editor and create a new file called DS.BAT.
2. Type *dosshell*.
3. Choose Save from the File menu, and then choose Exit.

That's it! You have created a batch file called DS.BAT and stored it in the root directory. Now instead of entering *dosshell* to load the Shell, you can enter *ds*. The new command is shorter, quicker to type, and harder to misspell.

Condensing commands Another advantage of batch files is that they enable you to condense a string of several commands into a single command. For example, if you do most of your work in a directory called C:\PROJECTS\ACCOUNTS\ CLIENTS, you can create a batch file to get you there quickly. Again working from the root directory, follow these steps:

1. Type *edit work.bat*, and press Enter to load the DOS Editor and create a new file called WORK.BAT.
2. Type *c:*, press Enter, and then type *cd \projects\accounts\clients*.
3. Save WORK.BAT, and exit the DOS Editor.

Now you can enter *work* (even from a drive other than drive C), and DOS will switch to drive C and make C:\PROJECTS\ACCOUNTS\CLIENTS the current directory.

Running applications   If you use one application program to perform most of your work, you can enhance WORK.BAT by including the name of the application program. If that application program is Microsoft Word, WORK.BAT looks like this:

c:
cd \projects\accounts\clients
word

Now entering *work* causes DOS to switch to drive C, make C:\PROJECTS\ACCOUNTS\CLIENTS the current directory, and run Microsoft Word.

You can run one program after another. For example, if you add another application program after **word**, that program will run automatically after you quit Word.

Running a series of programs

Loading files   You can enhance this batch file still further by using a *replaceable parameter*, which allows you to pass information to the batch file by including the information on

---

Batch-file discipline	**Create a batch-file directory**	**Using word processors**
Exercise a little restraint when using batch files to shorten command or program names. If you don't, before long you will have so many cryptic little batch files that even you won't remember what they do. Use batch files to shorten the names of programs you use frequently and avoid names someone (including you) might accidentally misstype. ♦	When you start using batch files and see how handy they can be, you will start to accumulate quite a collection of them. To keep things organized, put all your batch files in one directory and call it something appropriate (the name BATCH springs to mind). ♦	You can use your favorite word processor to create batch files as long as it allows you to save files without formatting information. Most popular word processors have this capability. ♦

the command line when you run the batch file. For example, you can add a replaceable parameter after the **word** program name in WORK.BAT so that Word automatically loads the file you specify following *work* on the command line.

Replaceable parameters →

In the batch file itself, you designate a replaceable parameter with a percent sign (%) followed by a number from 0 through 9. (A parameter of %0 always represents the name of the batch file; you'll probably use this parameter rarely.) A parameter of %1 represents the first item of information given on the command line after the batch file's name, a parameter of %2 represents the second item, and so on.

For the Word example above, you can add the replaceable parameter **%1** after the **word** program name in WORK.BAT so that Word automatically loads the file you type after *work* on the command line. After you add this parameter to the WORK.BAT batch file, the file looks like this:

c:
cd \projects\accounts\clients
word %1

To switch to drive C, make C:\PROJECTS\ACCOUNTS\ CLIENTS the current directory, run Microsoft Word, and load the file called SMITH.DOC, all you have to do is enter *work smith.doc*. DOS then substitutes SMITH.DOC for **%1** in the batch file.

Working with multiple files   Do you often need to run the same process on multiple files? The **for** command is designed for this purpose. This command has three required components: **for**, **in**, and **do**. (If you omit any of the components, DOS displays the error message *Syntax error* when you run the batch file.) The command is used in conjunction with a *replaceable variable* that is designated with two percent signs (%%) followed by a letter. DOS uses this variable to store the name of each file as it is processed.

Replaceable variables →

The best way to understand the **for** command is to look at an example. The following batch file, called FINDIT.BAT, uses the **for** command in conjunction with the **find** command to search for a series of text characters (known as a *text string*) in all the files in the current directory:

for %%p in (*.*) do find %1 %%p

To use FINDIT.BAT, you simply type *findit* followed by a string of characters enclosed in double quotation marks, and press Enter. Here's what the batch file does:

- **for** starts the process.
- **%%p** designates the replaceable variable DOS is to use for storing the name of each file as it is processed.
- **in (*.*)** specifies which files DOS is to process. In this case, you want DOS to search all the files in the current directory, so you use the * wildcard character to specify all files with all extensions. However, you could tell DOS to search a subset of files—for example, by specifying **in (*.txt)** to limit the search to all files with the TXT extension.
- **do** tells DOS to perform the following action on the files.
- **find %1 %%p** is that action. The syntax of the **find** command is **find** "*text_string*" *filename*—see page 124 for more information. When you run the batch file, DOS looks for the replaceable parameter %1 (the text string, which you type after the batch file's name on the command line) in the file whose name is stored in the replaceable variable **%%p**. DOS displays on the screen any lines that contain the characters you enter.

Here's an example of how you might use this batch file. Suppose you are a vendor of exercise equipment and you want to locate in your C:\PROJECTS\ACCOUNTS\CLIENTS directory all files with references to your line of weights.

Parameters vs. variables

Replaceable parameters and replaceable variables are easy to confuse. Replaceable parameters can be used with any batch file. They allow the batch file to use the words, phrases, or numbers (called *arguments*) that you type after the name of the batch file. Within the batch file, replaceable parameters are indicated by a % sign followed by a number from 0 through 9. The number in the batch file corresponds to the position of the argument after the batch-file name on the command line.

Replaceable variables are used only with the **for** command, and they hold the name of the file being processed. They are indicated by a single % sign if used from the command line or two % signs if used in batch files, followed by a single letter from *a* through *z*. ♦

Only one word

A single replaceable parameter can take only one word from the command line, so if you type in the batch-file example above, you can specify "weights" on the command line as the text string **find** should search for, but you cannot specify "weight bench". ♦

You create this batch file in the DOS Editor and save it with the name FINDIT.BAT. After quitting the Editor, you switch to the C:\PROJECTS\ACCOUNTS\CLIENTS directory, enter *findit "weights"*, and sit back while DOS methodically searches all the files, displaying the lines that contain the word *weights* on the screen.

Redirecting batch-file results

You can refine FINDIT.BAT by redirecting the output of the **find** command to a file called FINDIT.TXT. You need to use the >> redirection symbol to make sure the information from each successive file is appended to that of previous files, instead of overwriting existing information. With this refinement, FINDIT.BAT looks like this:

for %%p in (*.*) do find %1 %%p >> findit.txt

Before you run the new FINDIT.BAT, you must be sure to delete the existing FINDIT.TXT file. Otherwise, DOS tacks the results of this search onto the end of the results of old searches. The next section tells you how to fix this annoying problem.

Batch Files That Make Decisions

DOS provides some handy decision-making capabilities for batch files by means of the **if** command. The capabilities of the **if** command can be grouped into three catagories:

Three uses of the if command

- **if EXIST [*path*]*filename*** causes DOS to perform the actions specified after *filename* if that file exists.
- **if *string1==string2*** causes DOS to perform the actions specified after *string2* if one text string is the same as another text string.
- **if ERRORLEVEL** causes DOS to perform the actions specified after ERRORLEVEL if the return code from a prior command or program matches the number specified. When many programs (including some DOS commands) finish running, they return a code to DOS that indicates whether program execution was successful. Because DOS stores this return code under the name ERRORLEVEL, checking ERRORLEVEL allows DOS to decide whether to execute subsequent commands.

In each case, DOS tests whether the situation at hand meets the conditions described by the **if** command and if it does, performs the actions specified on the rest of the line. If the conditions are not met, DOS does not perform the specified actions but instead moves on to the next line of the batch file.

Let's look at some examples of how you can use the **if** command in conjunction with other commands.

Deleting an existing file   In the following example, we use the **if** command, replaceable parameters, and the **goto** command to modify the FINDIT.BAT batch file from the previous section so that it looks like this:

if not exist findit.txt goto proceed
del findit.txt
:proceed
for %%p in (*.*) do find %1 %%p >> findit.txt

With this batch file, you no longer have to check that you don't have an old copy of FINDIT.TXT in the directory. DOS checks for you. Here's what this batch file does:

- **if not exist findit.txt** tells DOS to check for the existence of FINDIT.TXT. If the file does not exist, DOS carries out the next command, **goto proceed**. The **goto** command enables you to jump over lines in the batch file and continue with the line that has the label specified in the command. In this case, if DOS doesn't find FINDIT.TXT, it jumps to the line labeled **:proceed**, skipping the second line of the batch file. However, if DOS does find FINDIT.TXT, it ignores the **goto** command and processes the second line of the batch file.

- **del findit.txt** tells DOS to delete FINDIT.TXT.

Skipping lines in a batch file

---

if NOT categories	**Return codes**	**string1==string2**
In addition to the three primary **if** categories, you can use the NOT operator to create these three secondary categories: **if NOT EXIST** [*path*]*filename* **if NOT** *string1==string2* **if NOT ERRORLEVEL** ♦	Many programs, upon completion, send a number to DOS. This number is referred to as a *return code*, an *error code*, or an *exit code*. A return code of 0 indicates the program completed without any problems. ♦	A couple of things to keep in mind when using the **if** command to test string equality: First, both strings must be enclosed in double quotation marks. Second, be aware that the comparison is case sensitive; that is, *flower*, *Flower*, and *FLOWER* are three different strings. ♦

Line labels

- **:proceed** is the line to which DOS jumps if FINDIT.TXT does not exist. The colon (:) at the beginning of the line tells DOS that **proceed** is a label and not a command.
- The fourth line of the batch file is the familiar instruction to search every file in the directory for the specified text string and report the results in FINDIT.TXT.

Running different programs If your work is divided between a spreadsheet program, a word-processing program, and a desktop-publishing program, you can use the following batch file, which we call LOAD.BAT, to take you to a specific directory and load an application program.

```
echo off
if "%1"=="" goto instructions
if "%1"=="l" goto spreadsheet
if "%1"=="w" goto wordprocessor
if "%1"=="v" goto publish
:spreadsheet
cd c:\lotus\accts
123
goto end
:wordprocessor
cd c:\word\documnts
word
goto end
:publish
cd c:\pub\write
vp
goto end
:instructions
echo Instructions: Use this batch file to work with
echo Lotus 1-2-3, Microsoft Word, or Ventura Publisher.
echo Type work followed by the appropriate letter.
echo          l - for Lotus 1-2-3
echo          w - for Microsoft Word
echo          v - for Ventura Publisher
:end
```

This batch file is quite a bit longer than the examples you have seen so far, but its sequence of simple commands is very easy to follow. You run the batch file by typing *load* followed by *l*, *w*, or *v* and pressing Enter. Here's what happens:

- **echo off** ensures that the following commands are not displayed on the screen.
- **if " %1"==... goto** ... checks whether you typed *l*, *w*, or *v* after *load* and jumps to the line in the batch file with the corresponding label. If you didn't type a letter to specify a particular application program to load, DOS jumps to the **instructions** label and tells you what the batch file does and what your choices are.
- The two commands that follow the **spreadsheet**, **word-processor**, and **publish** labels change directories and start an application program. When you quit the program and return to DOS, the batch file, which is still running, continues with the next line, **goto end**.
- **goto end** jumps over all the subsequent lines in the batch file to the line labeled **:end**.
- **echo** ... displays on the screen instructions for using this batch file. These instructions are displayed if you type *load* and press Enter without typing *l*, *w*, or *v*.
- **:end** allows the batch file to jump over the instruction lines when you quit the specified program. Because there are no more commands, the batch file ends.

You might want to use this batch file as a basis for one of your own, substituting your directories and program names.

Checking the ERRORLEVEL variable   Finally, let's look at an example of the **if** command that uses the ERRORLEVEL

Suppressing command display

---

echo and @

Use the **echo** command to suppress the display of commands in a batch file by adding this line at the beginning of the file

echo off

Use the @ sign at the beginning of a line to suppress display of that line. For example, preface the **echo off** command with an @ sign to eliminate its display. ♦

if "%1"==" "

Notice that you can specify what DOS should do if a replaceable parameter is not typed after the batch-file name. In the LOAD.BAT example shown above, if you enter *load* without an *l*, *w*, or *v*, the batch file jumps to the **instructions** label and displays instructions for how to use the batch file. ♦

rem

When you use the **rem** command in a batch file or your CONFIG.SYS file, DOS ignores any text that follows it. You use the **rem** command to add comments or descriptions to your batch files. Documenting what the batch file as a whole does, or what specific lines do, can be especially useful in long batch files or in batch files that you don't use frequently. ♦

variable. As we've already mentioned, DOS uses ERROR-LEVEL to record the return code (if any) of the previous process so that you can execute subsequent commands based on that process's success or failure. The tape backup program we use here at Online Press returns a code upon completion, and we use a batch file similar to this one to check whether the backup process was successfully completed:

```
@echo off
cd c:\tape
tape backup c:\projects\*.*="projects bkup"
if ERRORLEVEL==1 goto problems
echo everything O.K.
goto end
:problems
echo Backup not properly completed!!
:end
```

Here's what this batch file does:

- **@echo off** suppresses screen display of all commands (including itself) until an **echo** command turns the display back on. Used without the @ sign, this command suppresses the display of all commands except itself.
- **cd c:\tape** switches to the TAPE directory.
- **tape backup c:\projects*.*="projects bkup"** runs our tape backup program.
- **if ERRORLEVEL==1 goto problems** checks for an ERRORLEVEL that is equal to or greater than 1. Why use the value 1? Because by convention, a code of 0 indicates successful completion, and we are interested in situations in which the backup procedure was not successful. If ERRORLEVEL is equal to or greater than 1, the **goto** command tells DOS to jump to the line labeled **problems**.
- **echo everything O.K.** displays the message *everything O.K.* on the screen. This line is executed only if ERROR-LEVEL is equal to 0 (in other words, if the backup procedure was successful).
- **goto end** tells DOS to skip the remaining lines because the backup worked properly.
- **echo Backup not properly completed!!** tells DOS to display the message *Backup not properly completed!!* on the screen. The batch file reaches this point only if

ERRORLEVEL is equal to or greater than 1 (in other words, if the backup procedure was not successful).

As we mentioned earlier, many application programs return codes and so do some DOS commands. The DOS documentation calls these codes *exit codes* and indicates the commands that use exit codes as well as what each code means. Application programs usually document any return codes the program uses. Check the documentation under *return code*, *errorlevel code*, or *exit code*.

That's it for our quick course on batch files. As these few examples have demonstrated, batch files can be powerful tools. But remember, they don't have to be complicated or fancy, and almost anyone can make their work a little easier by using batch files.

Doskey

Doskey extends your control of the command line by enabling you to recall previous commands for reuse without having to type the command again. (For example, if you type a command incorrectly, you can recall it and edit it without retyping the whole thing.) Doskey also enables you to create and run *macros*.

You install Doskey by typing *doskey* on the command line and pressing Enter. You can also include the **doskey** command on a line by itself in your AUTOEXEC.BAT file so that the Doskey program is installed each time you turn on your computer. Doskey is a terminate-and-stay-resident program, meaning that it sits unseen in memory until you need to use it. The program takes up about 4 KB of conventional memory, and if you use many macros, you may need to use the /bufsize= switch with the **doskey** command to allocate more memory to accommodate them. After you have installed Doskey, the program keeps track of all the commands you enter at the command prompt and enables you to view the list of commands and recall any of them to the command line. Follow along with a short example to see how Doskey works:

Installing Doskey

1. Enter *doskey* to install the program. DOS responds with the message *Doskey installed*.

2. Now type *cls* and press Enter, type *dir c:\dos* and press Enter, and type *chkdsk* and press Enter.

Recalling commands

3. Display a list of the previously typed commands by pressing the F7 key. The list looks like this:

```
C:\>chkdsk
Volume Serial Number is 168F-6097

 33409024 bytes total disk space
    75776 bytes in 3 hidden files
    75776 bytes in 26 directories
 19369984 bytes in 1248 user files
    22528 bytes in bad sectors
 13864960 bytes available on disk

     2048 bytes in each allocation unit
    16313 total allocation units on disk
     6770 available allocation units on disk

   655360 total bytes memory
   589632 bytes free

C:\>
1: cls
2: dir c:\dos
3: chkdsk
C:\>
```

4. To recall the second command to the command line so that you can enter it again, press F9, and when Doskey prompts you for the line number of the command you want, press 2. Doskey displays *dir c:\dos* on the command line.

5. Modify the command so that it lists only files with the BAT extension, by adding *.bat* at the end of the command and pressing Enter.

6. Now press F7 again to see that *dir c:\dos*.bat* has been added to the list.

Using the F7 key to display the list of commands and the F9 key to specify the command you want is handy when you have entered many commands. If you have entered only a few commands or want to view only the commands you typed most recently, use the Up Arrow key to recall previous commands one at a time. For example, press F7, and then try pressing the Up Arrow key until the **cls** command is displayed. Use the Down Arrow key to work through the list in the opposite order, and use the Page Up and Page Down keys to jump to the top and bottom of the list.

Moving through the command list

Macros

Sometimes, *macro* seems like the lastest computer-industry buzzword, with different groups defining it in different ways. In the world of DOS, macros are like batch files in that both are collections of DOS commands. However, macros and batch files differ in these important ways:

- Macros run faster than batch files, because macros are stored in RAM, whereas batch files are stored on disk.
- The downside of RAM storage is that macros are lost when you turn off your machine, whereas batch files are preserved on your hard disk.
- Macros are made up of commands that you type on a single line, separating one command from the next with a paragraph-mark character. Batch files are made up of commands that you type on separate lines. The number of commands in a macro is limited by the maximum number of characters—127—that you can have on the command line, whereas batch files can contain an unlimited number of commands.
- You can use replaceable parameters in macros, but you specify them as $1 through $9 instead of %1 through %9. (Macros don't have an equivalent of %0.) You can also use redirection: The symbol $L is the equivalent of < in batch files, $G is the equivalent of >, and $B is the equivalent of |.
- Macros don't have decision-making capabilities.

No nested macros

Macros don't support the **call** command. Unlike batch files, which allow you to run one batch file from within another, macros cannot be run from within other macros. See page 112 for more information about using **call** in batch files. ◆

Ctrl-C

You can stop the execution of a batch file by pressing Ctrl-C. You can stop a macro in the same way. However, if the macro consists of multiple commands, you must press Ctrl-C for each command in the macro. ◆

Multiple commands

With Doskey installed, you can type multiple commands on a single line. To separate the commands, press Ctrl-T to insert a paragraph-mark character. For example, the macro

md wrk¶copy *.doc wrk

creates a directory called WRK and copies all the files with a DOC extension to it. ◆

Creating macros Macros are easy to create. For example, to create a macro that redirects the output of the **type** command to the **more** command so that DOS displays the text of a specified file one screenful at a time, follow these steps:

1. Type *doskey* followed by the name you want to assign the macro. For example, type *doskey tp* (for *type page*).
2. Type an equal sign to separate the macro name from the first DOS command in the macro.
3. Next, type *type* (the **type** command), a space, $1 (the replaceable parameter for the name of the file to be displayed), another space, the $B redirection symbol (the equivalent of |), another space, and *more* (the **more** command).
4. Finish the macro by pressing Enter.

The result looks like this:

doskey tp=type $1 $B more

From now until you turn off your computer, all you have to do to view any file a screenful at a time is type *tp* followed by the name of the file and press Enter. DOS then substitutes the name for the $1 parameter in the macro and redirects the output from the **type** command to the **more** command, which displays the file a screenful at a time.

Preserving macros Creating macros only to lose them as soon as you turn off your machine can get tiresome, especially if you regularly use the same macros. The easiest way to save macros from session to session is in a batch file. To save all the macros currently in RAM, simply enter

Saving as a batch file

doskey /macros > macro.bat

DOS then stores the macros in a file called MACRO.BAT. But before you can use the MACRO.BAT file to reload these macros, you must load the MACRO.BAT file into an editor and add the word *doskey* in front of each macro definition. With that done, you can load the stored macros into memory by typing *macro* at the command prompt and pressing Enter, or by adding *macro* to your AUTOEXEC.BAT file.

Macros vs. batch files As we have seen, macros are much like batch files. When should you use a macro and when should you use a batch file? If you need decision-making capabilities, you have no choice: You must use batch files, because macros don't have these capabilities. Length is another consideration: Macros are limited to 127 characters, whereas batch files can be as long as you need them to be. Macros, with their greater speed, work well for short, often-used commands. Variations of existing commands, like the *tp* macro, are good candidates.

Optimizing Your System

Having discussed what you can do at the command level to increase your productivity, let's turn our attention to ways in which you can optimize your computer's performance. Several optimization strategies are available to you. Some are simple and cheap; others are complex and expensive. What's more, some methods help one type of computer and hinder another. Although specific techniques and technical solutions are beyond the scope of this book, in this section we'll try to help you sort out the possibilities and direct you to those that promise the best results.

Your Computer

All the fine-tuning in the world can't turn a Model T into a Ferrari. The same is true in the computer world. That old XT will never run like a new 486 machine, regardless of what you might do.

If you are using a computer based on an 80286 or earlier chip, you might gain significantly by upgrading to a machine based on an 80386 or 80486 chip. These machines have much more raw processing power and, perhaps more importantly, contemporary software is written to take advantage of the additional capabilities of these new chips. However, millions of users get all they need from 80286 machines. Consider upgrading only if you know that the programs you need to run are not operating at their full potential.

Memory

Short of buying a new machine, adding memory (RAM) is probably the next best method of improving performance. As we mentioned in Chapter 1, most computers come with

640 KB of RAM that is known as *conventional memory*. Computers based on the 80286 and later chips can also have *extended memory*, which comes in the form of chips or modules that are inserted into vacant sockets on your computer's motherboard. They can also have *expanded memory*, which comes in the form of a board that is installed in a vacant slot in your computer's motherboard. Expanded memory has been available longer than extended memory, but the latter is now the preferred method of adding more memory to a machine.

Memory managers

Many programs are unable to use added extended or expanded memory without the assistance of a program called a *memory manager*. A memory manager makes the additional memory accessible and eliminates conflicting memory requests. One of the significant advantages of DOS 5 over earlier versions is the incorporation of memory-management programs. We briefly discuss these programs later in this chapter.

Math Coprocessors

Math coprocessors make computers run faster. Like extended-memory chips and an expanded-memory board, a math coprocessor is hardware that must be installed in your machine. Some application programs—for example, most computer-aided design (CAD) programs—won't run on computers that do not have coprocessors. But many programs can't take advantage of them. The benefits of adding a coprocessor are highly contingent on the type of application programs you use. Programs that spend most of their time calculating (CAD programs, graphics programs, and some spreadsheets) are most likely to get a performance boost from a coprocessor.

Strategies That Don't Cost Money

So you don't want to buy a new computer or spend $300 to $1000 to add memory or a coprocessor to your old one? Let's survey some of the tools that come with DOS 5 to boost your current machine's performance.

Before we get started, you should know that the DOS 5 installation program does quite a good job of evaluating the capabilities of your computer and installing itself in the most advantageous manner. Most of the fine-tuning you can do to your system involves tinkering with your AUTOEXEC.BAT and CONFIG.SYS files.

Before you implement any of the suggestions in this section, you should make a system disk that includes copies of your AUTOEXEC.BAT and CONFIG.SYS files, by following these steps:

1. Insert a formatted, blank floppy disk in drive A, and enter *sys a:*. The **sys** command copies IO.SYS and MSDOS.SYS (the two hidden system files) and COMMAND.COM to the floppy disk.

2. Now create a directory called FILES on the floppy disk.

3. Next, switch to the root directory of drive C. At the command prompt, type *copy config.sys a:\files*, and press Enter. Finally, type *copy autoexec.bat a:\files*, and press Enter.

Creating a system disk

Now if the alterations you make to these files on your hard disk prevent your computer from booting properly, you can insert the floppy disk, start your computer using the old versions of the files, and then copy the old AUTOEXEC.BAT and CONFIG.SYS files to your hard disk.

With these two critical files safely stowed away on floppy disk, you are free to experiment. The following sections briefly introduce some of the options open to you, but detailed instructions about using these options is beyond the scope of this book. See the documentation if you need more information.

Memory managers   DOS 5 includes two memory-management programs that can be used with computers based on the 80286, 80386, or 80486 chip that have some form of additional memory (extended or expanded).

- HIMEM makes extended memory available to programs that can use it.

- EMM386 works only on 80386 and 80486 systems and lets you use extended memory to emulate expanded memory. Some application programs can take advantage only of expanded memory. In effect, EMM386 converts extended memory to expanded memory, allowing you to run these programs.

If your system has extended memory, these two programs allow you to run DOS 5 in extended memory, thereby freeing conventional memory for application program use.

Loading programs into upper memory   If you have an 80386 or 80486-based machine with extended memory, the DOS 5 installation program is smart enough to detect the added memory and will automatically load part of DOS into the extended memory. To free up even more conventional memory, you might be able to load some device drivers and terminate-and-stay-resident (TSR) programs into *upper memory*, an area of memory between conventional memory and extended memory.

Most of upper memory is used for system processes, but blocks of this memory often go unused. To use this area of memory, you must install the EMM386 memory manager. Detailed instructions on installing EMM386 and running programs in upper memory are beyond the scope of this book but can be found in the DOS 5 documentation.

Using a RAM disk   A RAM disk, also called a *virtual drive* or *virtual disk*, is a part of memory that emulates a physical hard disk. You use a RAM disk like any other drive on your computer, but because it is an area of memory and not a physical disk, information transfer to and from the RAM disk is very fast.

Although you can construct a RAM disk from conventional memory, this technique is really practical only if you have some form of add-in memory (extended or expanded). Detailed instructions for creating a RAM disk are beyond the scope of this book, but now that you know such a technique is possible, you might want to explore the documentation for more information.

A warning about RAM disks: Their contents are lost when you turn off your computer or if the power goes out. Use the RAM disk to process data, but store the files on your physical hard drive.

Improving file access speed   DOS 5 comes with a program called Fastopen that you can use to speed up access to previously opened files. When you run Fastopen, the program stores the names and locations of the files you open during any particular work session. Subsequent access to these files is faster because Fastopen already knows where the files are located. Fastopen is most likely to speed things up if you use database programs or language compilers.

As with most of the optimization strategies, try Fastopen and see if it makes you more efficient. If you don't notice a difference, stop using Fastopen to free up the memory it uses. A couple of other warnings about Fastopen:

- Fastopen doesn't work over a network.
- Don't run Fastopen from the DOS Shell. It may freeze your computer.
- Never use a disk-defragmentation program while Fastopen is loaded. You could lose data.

We can't go into detail about installing and using Fastopen here; see the documentation for more information.

Reducing disk access with SMARTdrive   Like Fastopen, the SMARTdrive program stores information. SMARTdrive, however, stores actual data read from the hard drive. This data goes into an area of memory called the *SMARTdrive cache*, and the next time a program tries to read that data from the hard drive, SMARTdrive intercepts the data request and loads the data from its cache instead. As a result, access to the data is much faster. You must have some form of add-in memory (extended or expanded) to use SMARTdrive, and you cannot run another disk-caching program concurrently. See the documentation for more information about this productivity tool.

Other Suggestions

The following routine procedures will help keep your optimized machine humming efficiently:

- Delete unnecessary files. If your hard drive is packed with programs or data files that you don't use now but might need in the future, back them up and erase them from your hard disk.
- Run a disk-defragmentation program regularly. Keeping files contiguous makes loading them faster. See page 78 for more information.

- Run the **chkdsk** command regularly. You will then be aware of lost clusters on your hard drive. (Most disk-defragmentation utilities will also point out these problems. They cannot, however, fix the problems they find.) See page 79 for more information.
- Keep the **path** command in your AUTOEXEC.BAT file short, and put the most frequently used directories at the beginning of the command. This strategy helps reduce the time DOS takes to find files.

After reading this chapter, you should have some ideas about how to make your time in front of the computer more productive. You might create batch files or macros to automate tedious jobs. Or perhaps adding a RAM drive or installing SMARTDrive will be your ticket to more work completed in less time.

6

The DOS Tools
at a Glance

E ven though we have covered a lot of ground in the preceding chapters, there is still much more to DOS. We designed this last chapter with that thought in mind. We asked ourselves how we could help you identify the particular DOS command you need to perform a specific task. The answer is the table at the beginning of this chapter. Then we asked ourselves how we could give you an idea of the overall scope of DOS commands, perhaps inspiring you to try using DOS in ways you had never thought of before. The answer is the handy alphabetical reference that makes up the bulk of this chapter.

Table of Common Tasks

The following table is for those times when you know what you want to do but can't remember the DOS command that accomplishes that particular task. We list common tasks in seven categories: basic tasks, basic Shell tasks, batch-file tasks, disk and directory tasks, file tasks, maintenance and troubleshooting tasks, and system-configuration tasks. Included in the table are the name of the command you use, the equivalent Shell procedure (if any), and the page in this chapter where you can obtain more information. This table is not intended to be all-inclusive. You will perform some of the listed tasks every day; you may never need to perform others, particularly those listed in the system-configuration section.

Task	Command	Shell	Page
Basic Tasks			
Clear the screen	**cls**	*	114
Display information a screenful at a time	**more**	*	130
Display or change the system date	**date**	*	116
Display or change the system time	**time**	*	138
Display the DOS version number	**ver**	*	141
Get online help about DOS commands	**help**	Commands (Help menu)	126
Load QBasic	**qbasic**	MS-DOS QBasic (Program List area)	133
Load the Shell	**dosshell**	*	120
Put several commands on one command line	**doskey**	*	120
Recall previously used commands	**doskey**	*	120
Create DOS macros	**doskey**	*	120

Task	Command	Shell	Page
Set or display a path	**path**	*	131

Basic Shell Tasks

Task	Command	Shell	Page
Change the color scheme of the Shell		Colors (Options menu)	
Disable confirmation dialog boxes		Confirmation (Options menu)	55
Display areas of the Shell in greater detail		View menu	17
Enable confirmation dialog boxes		Confirmation (Options menu)	55
Expand or shrink the Directory Tree area		Tree menu	17
Get help in the Shell		Help menu	21
Load the Shell	**dosshell**		120
Quit the Shell		F3; Exit (File menu)	24
Return to the Shell from the command line	**exit**		122
Switch between text and graphics mode		Display (Options menu)	13
Update the Shell screen		Refresh (View menu)	38

Batch-File Tasks

Task	Command	Shell	Page
Direct DOS to a specific batch-file line	**goto**	*	126
Do different things depending on the situation	**if**	*	127
Include comments	**rem**	*	134
Run a batch file from within a batch file	**call**	*	112
Suppress command display	**echo**	*	120
Temporarily halt batch-file execution	**pause**	*	131

Disk and Directory Tasks

Task	Command	Shell	Page
Assign a different drive letter	**assign**	*	110
Check for lost clusters	**chkdsk**	*	113
Compare contents of two floppy disks	**diskcomp**	*	119
Copy contents of a disk	**diskcopy**	Disk Utilities (Program List area)	119
Copy an entire directory	**xcopy**	*	142
Create a system or bootable disk	**sys**	*	138
Create a new directory	**md**	Create Directory (File menu)	128
Create or modify a volume label	**label**	*	127
Delete a directory	**rd**	Highlight and press Delete key	133
Display information about partitions	**fdisk**	*	124
Display the directory structure of a path or disk	**tree**	Directory Tree area	139
Display a volume label	**vol**	*	142
Format a disk	**format**	Disk Utilities (Program List area)	125

* You cannot use this command directly from the Shell. You must enter this command at the command prompt. Press Shift-F9, choose Run from the File menu, or select Command Prompt in the Program List area to load a copy of COMMAND.COM and display the command prompt. Then enter the command, and move back to the Shell by using the **exit** command.

Task	Command	Shell	Page
Get a disk status report	**chkdsk**	*	113
Protect disks from accidental formatting	**mirror**	*	129
Substitute a drive letter for a path	**subst**	*	137
Switch to another directory	**cd**	Click or tab to desired directory	113
Treat a drive as a directory	**join**	*	127
Treat files in a specified directory as if they were in the current directory	**append**	*	110
Unformat an accidentally formatted disk	**unformat**	*	140

File Tasks

Task	Command	Shell	Page
Add a file to a directory	**replace**	*	134
Back up files to a different disk	**backup**	Disk Utilities (Program List area)	112
Change a filename	**ren**	Rename (File menu)	134
Combine files	**copy**	*	115
Compare contents of two or more files	**comp; fc**	*	123
Copy all files in a directory and its subdirectories	**xcopy**	*	142
Copy a file	**copy**	Copy (File menu)	115
Copy files based on date	**xcopy**	*	142
Copy a file to a device	**copy**	*	115
Delete a file	**del**	Delete (File menu)	117
Deselect all files in a directory		Deselect All (File menu)	48
Display filenames in a directory	**dir**	Click or tab to that directory	118
Display files based on wildcard specification or filename	**dir**	File Display Options (Options menu)	118
Display information about a file	**dir**	Show Information (Options menu)	118
Display or set file attributes	**attrib**	Change Attribute (File menu)	114
Display contents of a text file	**type**	View File Contents (File menu)	139
Find specific text within a file	**find**	*	124
Link an extension with a program		Associate (File menu)	65
Load files into the associated program		Open (File menu)	65
Look for a file	**dir**	Search (File menu)	118
Move files from one directory to another		Move (File menu)	
Print a file	**copy; print**	Print (File menu)	115 131
Protect files from accidental deletion	**mirror**	*	129
Recover an accidentally deleted file	**undelete**	Disk Utilities (Program List area)	140
Rename a file	**ren**	Rename (File menu)	134
Replace a file with a file of same name	**replace**	*	134

Task	Command	Shell	Page
Restore files	**restore**	Disk Utilities (Program List area)	135
Run a program	Type program name	Open (File menu)	
Select all files in a directory	Use *.*	Select All (File menu)	48
Select files from more than one directory		Select Across Directories (Options menu)	
Sort information	**sort**	*	136
Speed up access time to previously opened files	**fastopen**	*	123
Switch from one application to another		Enable Task Swapper (Options menu)	65
Tell DOS which directories to search for files	**path**	*	131
Use the DOS Editor	**edit**	Editor (Program List area)	121
Verify that a file is correctly written to disk	**copy;** **verify**	*	115 141

Maintenance and Troubleshooting Tasks

Task	Command	Shell	Page
Determine amount of free memory	**mem**	*	128
Examine where programs are loaded in memory	**mem**	*	128
Expand (decompress) DOS 5 files	**expand**	*	122
Extract information from a defective disk	**recover**	*	133

System-Configuration Tasks

Task	Command	Shell	Page
Set the version number DOS 5 sends to a program	**setver**	*	136
Check for Ctrl-C as frequently or as infrequently as possible	**break**	*	110
Configure a printer, device, or port	**mode**	*	130
Display more or fewer lines per screen	**mode**	*	130
Enable expanded-memory support for 386 machines	**emm386**	*	122
Enable file-sharing and file-locking on your system	**share**	*	136
Enable printing of color or graphics screens	**graphics**	*	126
Increase environment space	**shell**	*	110
Load device drivers into upper memory	**devicehigh**	*	110
Load DOS into high memory	**dos**	*	110
Load memory-resident programs upon startup	**install**	*	110
Load a program into upper memory	**loadhigh**	*	128
Modify the command prompt	**prompt**	*	110
Specify a device driver to load into memory	**device**	*	110
Specify a location for the command interpreter	**shell**	*	110
Specify the number of accessible drives	**lastdrive**	*	110

* You cannot use this command directly from the Shell. You must enter this command at the command prompt. Press Shift-F9, choose Run from the File menu, or select Command Prompt in the Program List area to load a copy of COMMAND.COM and display the command prompt. Then enter the command, and move back to the Shell by using the **exit** command.

Alphabetical Command Reference

Check the following reference when you forget the syntax of a command or how to use it. (We tell you how to read syntax diagrams on page 26.) For those commands we think you'll use most often, we present a situation you might encounter or a task you might need to perform and show you how to use a DOS command to achieve the desired result. This "Ann Landers" problem/solution approach might help you see how you can apply DOS commands to your work in ways you might not have thought of before.

Because some DOS commands are specialized or technical, this reference is not intended to be comprehensive. For example, we don't give details about the commands for using languages other than English, because most people will never use these commands. We offer only a short description, in case you are curious about what such commands do.

We have omitted from the reference the following commands that are used in the CONFIG.SYS file:

break	**devicehigh**	**files**	**stacks**
buffers	**dos**	**install**	**switches**
country	**drivparm**	**lastdrive**	
device	**fcbs**	**shell**	

Also omitted are commands that appear only on Shell menus.

You might want to browse through this reference, looking for ideas about how to make your work faster or easier. Some of the more specialized DOS commands might turn out to be perfect for a job you need to do.

append

append [[*drive*:]*path*[;...]] [/x[:on|:off]] [/path:on|/path:off] [/e]

Use the **append** command to make DOS treat files in other directories as if they were in the current directory.

assign

assign [x[:]=y[:][...]]

Use the **assign** command to switch requests from one disk drive to another. You'll probably want to use the **subst** command instead of **assign**. (We discuss **subst** on page 137.)

attrib

Improved in DOS 5

attrib [+*attribute* | –*attribute*] [[*drive:*][*path*]*filename*] [/s]

When to Use

You have written a report that contains sensitive information and you don't want other people to know that the report exists on your hard drive.

A spreadsheet used by your company to project profits can be viewed but not changed. Now you need to update a formula in the file.

Use the **attrib** (Attribute) command to hide the report and remove the read-only attribute from the spreadsheet.

You can turn four attributes on or off with this command, preceding them with a + sign to turn them on and with a – sign to turn them off.

- The h (hidden) attribute makes a file invisible to the **dir**, **copy**, **xcopy**, **rename**, and **delete** commands.
- The r (read-only) attribute protects a file from being changed. The file can be viewed but cannot be altered.
- The a (archive) attribute indicates whether a file has been changed since it was last backed up.
- The s (system) attribute labels the file as a system file and also hides it.

How to Use

See what attributes are assigned to the 1ST_QTR.RPT file by entering

attrib 1st_qtr.rpt

Hide the 1ST_QTR.RPT file by entering

attrib +h 1st_qtr.rpt

Hide all files with the RPT extension by entering

attrib +h *.rpt

Remove the read-only attribute from the spreadsheet called PROFIT.SUM by entering

attrib –r profit.sum

backup

backup *source destination_drive*: [/s] [/m] [/a] [/f[:*size*]]
　　[/d:*date*[/t:*time*]] [/l[:[*drive*:][*path*]*logfile*]]

When to Use

You need to back up a file that is 1.6 MB—too large to fit on a high-density, 5.25-inch floppy disk.

You need to back up all the files in the current directory that have been worked on since June 1, 1991.

Use the **backup** command to copy the large file to more than one floppy disk and to back up large numbers of files. (The **copy** or **xcopy** command might be more suitable for backing up small amounts of data.) To restore files backed up with the **backup** command, you must use the **restore** command.

See page 61 for details about **backup** and page 62 for details about **restore**.

How to Use

Back up a 1.6 MB file called ANNUAL.RPT on floppy disks by entering

　　backup annual.rpt a:

and inserting a new disk when DOS requests one.

Back up all the files in the current directory that are dated after June 1, 1991 by entering

　　backup *.* a: /d:06-01-91

call

call [*drive*:][*path*]*filename* [*batch-parameters*]

Use the **call** command in a batch file to start a second batch file and then return to the first one. The *filename* parameter (the second batch file) must have a BAT extension. The *batch-parameters* parameter is any information that you normally type after the second batch file's name on the command line.

cd or chdir

cd [*drive:*][*path*]
chdir [*drive:*][*path*]

Use the **cd** (Change Directory) command to move to another directory (**chdir** is an alternative form of this command). This command is covered in detail on page 42.

chcp

chcp [*nnn*]

Use the **chcp** command to change the active code page, which is one of a number of changes you need to make if you want to use a language other than English. See the DOS documentation for more information.

chkdsk

chkdsk [*drive:*][*path*]*filename*] [/f] [/v]

When to Use

You notice that the free space on your hard disk is decreasing, even though you haven't saved any files lately.

Your 4-year-old son turns off your machine while you are using your word processor.

Use the **chkdsk** (Check Disk) command to check for errors in a disk's file system. It pays to run **chkdsk** regularly to be sure your hard disk is free from error and to prevent possible loss of data. The **chkdsk** command verifies that all files are where they are supposed to be and that they are the correct size. If you include the /f switch in the **chkdsk** command, DOS reconciles any errors it finds.

See page 79 for more information about **chkdsk**.

How to Use

Your missing disk space might be in the form of lost clusters (data that is on the hard disk but not accounted for in the FAT). Tell DOS to analyze the disk by entering:

chkdsk

Switching off your computer while application programs are running might damage the FAT. Use the **chkdsk** command as described above to ascertain the extent of the damage.

cls

cls

When to Use

Your screen is filled with previously typed commands, and you want to erase the clutter.

When you exit a game program, the screen is still the bright green color that the game uses.

Use the **cls** command to clear the screen and reposition the prompt.

How to Use

No parameters or switches here. Simply type the command:

cls

command

command [[*drive:*]*path*][*device*] [/e:*nnnnn*] [/p] [/c *string*] [/msg]

When to Use

You have just tried to run a program and DOS displayed the message "Out of environment space."

Use the **command** command to increase the environment space, load a second copy of COMMAND.COM, or specify a new location for COMMAND.COM.

How to Use

Increase your environment space by using the **command** command in conjunction with the **shell** command:

shell=c:\dos\command.com /e:512 /p

The number following the /e switch indicates the size of the environment.

comp

comp [*data1*] [*data2*] [/d] [/a] [/l] [/n=*number*] [/c]

The **comp** command compares two files byte by byte, abandoning the comparison operation as soon as it locates a difference between the two files.

Generally, you will want to use the **fc** command instead of the **comp** command. The **fc** command compares the files and reports any differences it finds. See page 123 for more information about the **fc** command.

copy

copy [/a|/b] *source* [/a|/b] [+ *source* [/a|/b] [+...]] [*destination* [/a|/b] [/v]

When to Use

You want to join the files for the 1st, 2nd, 3rd, and 4th quarters into one annual-report file.

Use the **copy** command to copy files, copy and rename files with one command, join files, or send a file to a device (usually a printer). You can use the /a switch to specify that the file you are copying is in ASCII format and the /b switch to specify that the file is in binary format. Page 49 gives detailed information about common uses of the **copy** command. Here, we cover only the use of **copy** to join, or *concatenate*, files.

How to Use

Join four quarterly-report files into one annual-report file by entering

> **copy 1st_qtr.rpt + 2nd_qtr.rpt + 3rd_qtr.rpt
> + 4th_qtr.rpt annual.rpt**

DOS joins the four quarterly-report files in the annual-report file in the order you specified on the command line.

ctty

ctty *device*

Use the **ctty** command to change the terminal device used to control your system. For more information on this specialized command, see the documentation.

date

date [*mm-dd-yy*]

When to Use

You have an older computer that does not store the date and time. Some days, you forget to set the date before starting work, and all the files you create then have Jan 1, 1980 as their creation date, making it impossible to determine which is the most up-to-date file.

You want to ensure that you do not forget to enter the date when you turn on your computer.

Use the **date** command to display the current date, as recorded by your computer's clock, and to change the date, if necessary.

If you have an older IBM PC, XT, or compatible, your computer may not store the date and time automatically. In that case, you will need to set the date and time each time you turn on the computer so that the application programs you use can assign accurate creation and modification dates to the files you work with. Otherwise, all the files will have the default date (Jan 1, 1980). Adding the **date** command to your AUTOEXEC.BAT file prompts you to enter the current date before doing any work.

How to Use

Change the date to June 1, 1991 by entering

> **date 06-01-91**

Tell DOS to prompt you to enter the date by loading your AUTOEXEC.BAT file into the DOS Editor (see page 29), entering

> **date**

on a line by itself, and saving the file. The next time you boot your computer, DOS displays the date stored by your computer's clock and prompts you to enter a new date. If you don't want to change the displayed date, simply press Enter.

debug

debug [[*drive:*][*path*]*filename* [*testfile-parameters*]]
See the documentation for more information.

When to Use

You recently noticed a small assembly-language utility in a computer magazine, and you would like to be able to use the utility.

Use the **debug** command for assembling program code, patching existing program files, examining memory, and other technical functions. Note: **debug** is an advanced command and can corrupt memory if used incorrectly.

How to Use

Enter the program code from the magazine into a file using **debug** or a text editor. Refer to the documentation for the specific switches needed to save and assemble the program.

del

del [*drive:*][*path*]*filename* [/p]

When to Use

You have renamed old files with an OLD extension, and now you want to delete them.

You want to delete all the files with a DOC extension in the current directory, with the exception of two specific files.

Use the **del** command to erase file(s) from a disk. This command works with a single file or with multiple files specified with wildcards. If you accidentally delete files you need, use the **undelete** command to recover them.

See page 52 for more information about **del** and page 68 for more information about **undelete**.

How to Use

Erase the old files by entering

del *.old

Use the **del** command with the /p switch to have DOS ask you to confirm that it should delete a file, like this:

del *.doc /p

*Improved
in DOS 5*

dir

dir [*drive:*][*path*][*filename*] [/p] [/w] [/a[[:]*attributes*]]
　　[/o[[:]*sortorder*]] [/s] [/b] [/l]

When to Use

**You want to view the contents of a directory that contains
many files, but every time you enter the dir command, the list
scrolls by too fast for you to see the filenames.**

**You've forgotten the name of the file you want to load, but
you know that it is a read-only file. You want to quickly scan
all read-only filenames to pinpoint the one you need.**

Use the **dir** (Directory) command to display the names, sizes,
and creation dates of the files in a specific directory. By using
the command's many switches, either alone or in various
combinations, you can vary its output in many useful ways.

- Use the /p switch to display a screenful of information
  at a time.
- Use the /w switch to display the filenames (without size
  or date information) in rows across the screen.
- Use the /a switch to display the filenames of all files
  with the specified attribute.
- Use the /o switch to change the order in which files are
  displayed. Displaying files by date is often useful for
  determining the most recent version of a file. (See the
  documentation for a list of the different search orders
  possible.)
- Use the /s switch to search the current directory and its
  subdirectories for occurrences of the file(s) you specify.
  Search an entire drive by moving to the root directory
  before invoking the command.
- Use the /b switch to display directory names and filenames without header or summary information.
- Use the /l switch to display directory listings in lowercase.

How to Use
Display information about the files in the current directory
one screen at a time by entering

　　dir /p

Display all the read-only files in the current directory by entering

dir /a:r

Other possible attributes include hidden, system, and archive.

diskcomp

diskcomp [*drive1*:[*drive2*:]] [/1] [/8]

When to Use

You want to be sure that two floppy disks contain identical files stored in identical directory structures, but you have only one floppy disk drive.

Use the **diskcomp** (Disk Compare) command to compare the contents of two floppy disks.

You will probably never use the two optional switches, /1 and /8, which compare only the first sides of the disks or the first eight sectors per track.

How to Use

Compare the contents of two floppy disks on a machine with only one floppy disk drive by entering

diskcomp a: a:

DOS instructs you to insert each disk in drive A as needed.

diskcopy

diskcopy [*drive1*:[*drive2*:]] [/1] [/v]

When to Use

You want to make a copy of an application program you have just purchased so that you can store the original disks in a safe place and use the copies to install the program on your computer.

Use the **diskcopy** command to copy the contents of one floppy disk to another. Use the /1 switch to copy only the first side of the disk and the /v switch to have DOS verify that the information was copied correctly. Note that the source disk and target disk need to have the same storage capacity and that the target disk must be formatted.

How to Use

Copy the disks by entering

   diskcopy a: a:

DOS prompts you to insert the source disk and copies its contents into memory. It then prompts you to replace the source disk with the target disk and copies the source-disk information from memory to the target disk.

doskey

*New
in DOS 5*

doskey [/reinstall] [/bufsize=*size*] [/macros] [/history]
   [/insert|/overstrike] [*macroname*=[text]]

Use the **doskey** command to recall a previous command line so that you can edit and reuse it and to load the Doskey program. Doskey is a terminate-and-stay-resident (TSR) program that also enables you to create macros—sets of DOS commands that you run at the same time to accomplish specific tasks and that you store in memory under a single name. Entering the name of the macro tells DOS to carry out all the commands. See pages 95 and 97 for more information about Doskey and macros.

dosshell

*New
in DOS 5*

dosshell [/t[:*res*[*n*]]] [/b]
dosshell [/g[:*res*[*n*]]] [/b]

Use the **dosshell** command to load the DOS Shell. You can specify that the Shell be loaded in text mode (/t) or graphics mode (/g), and you can specify that the screen be in black-and-white (/b) and a specific resolution (*res*[*n*]). See Chapter 2 for details about the Shell.

echo

echo [on|off]

Use the **echo** command in batch files to display the commands in the batch file on the screen (*echo on*) or suppress the display of commands (*echo off*).

edit

edit [[*drive*:][*path*][*filename*]] [/b] [/g] [/h] [/nohi]

New in DOS 5

When to Use

You want to create a simple list of accounts that you can refer to as a memory jogger without having to load an application program.

Use the **edit** command to load the DOS Editor, a handy tool for creating batch files or notes that don't require fancy formatting. The **edit** command has four switches:

- The /b switch displays the editor in black and white.
- The /g switch enhances performance on a CGA monitor.
- The /h switch causes the editor to display the maximum number of lines possible for your monitor.
- The /nohi switch, which you'll probably never use, enables use of 8-color monitors.

Note that you cannot use the DOS Editor if QBasic is not in the current directory or a directory in the **path** command.

How to Use

Load the DOS Editor and at the same time create a new file called ACCOUNTS.LST in the current directory by entering

edit accounts.lst

Enter the list of accounts and then save the file by choosing Save from the File menu. Choose Exit to return to the command prompt.

edlin

edlin [*drive*:][*path*]*filename* [/b]

Use the **edlin** command to load Edlin, a text editor. Edlin was the only editor included with previous versions of DOS, but now that the DOS Editor is available, you will probably never use Edlin. (You use the **edit** command, discussed above, to load the DOS Editor.)

New
in DOS 5

emm386

emm386 [on|off|auto] [w=on|w=off]

Use the **emm386** command for a variety of tasks related to memory management in computers based on the 80386 or higher CPU. See the documentation for more information.

exe2bin

exe2bin [*drive1*:][*path1*]*input-file* [[*drive2*:][*path2*]*output-file*]

Use this utility to convert a properly designed EXE program to a binary file (probably a file with a COM extension). It is useful only to programmers. See the documentation for more information.

exit

exit

Use the **exit** command to get back to the Shell from a command line invoked by pressing Shift F9. From the Shell, you can execute DOS commands by pressing Shift-F9 to load another copy of COMMAND.COM. After you complete your tasks on the command line, you cannot return to the Shell until you exit this copy of COMMAND.COM. See page 24 for information about switching between the Shell and the command line.

expand

expand [*drive*:][*path*]*filename* [[*drive*:][*path*]*filename*[...]] *destination*

When to Use

The HIMEM.SYS memory-management program has been accidentally erased from your hard disk, and you need to load another copy of the file from your DOS disks.

Most of the programs on the DOS 5 disks are compressed. (The extensions of compressed files end with an underscore character.) To copy programs from these DOS 5 disks in a usable format, use the **expand** command to expand the compressed files as they are copied.

How to Use

Copy and expand a new copy of HIMEM.SYS by inserting the DOS disk that holds the file and entering

expand a:\himem.sy_ c:\dos\himem.sys

fastopen

fastopen *drive*:[[=]*n*] [*drive*:[[=]*n*][...]] [/x]

Use the **fastopen** command to greatly reduce the time necessary to access files and directories.

Fastopen is a performance-enhancing program. It keeps track of the files and directories you open and allows speedy subsequent access to those files and directories. Using this program has advantages and disadvantages. See the documentation for more information.

fc

fc [/a] [/c] [*drive1*:][*path1*]*filename1* [*drive2*:][*path2*]*filename2*
See the documentation for information about other parameters and
    switches.

When to Use

You sent both a printout and a disk file of a proposal to a colleague for comment. He made some changes to the disk file but didn't indicate them on the printout. You need a quick way of comparing the file you sent him with the one he returned.

Use the **fc** command to compare the two files and make a list of any differences between them.

How to Use

Change the name or extension of one of the files (see page 51 for information about renaming files), copy both files to the current directory, and then compare them by entering

fc proposal.old proposal.new

DOS compares the files and displays on the screen any lines that differ.

If you want a record of the differences, redirect the output of **fc** from the screen to a file called COMPARE.TXT by entering

fc proposal.old proposal.new > compare.out

For more information on redirection, see page 82.

fdisk

fdisk

Use the **fdisk** (Format Disk) command to create, delete, and modify partitions on a hard disk.

Running **fdisk** is a simple matter of typing the command name, but be warned: Changing partition information can lead to loss of data. See the documentation for important information about **fdisk**.

find

find [/v] [/c] [/n] [/i] *"string"* [[*drive*:][*path*]*filename* [...]]

When to Use

You want to check that you have used the word *affect* **correctly in the file called IMPACT.DOC.**

Use the **find** command to search a file for words or phrases (text strings). The results of the command vary depending on which switches you use.

- The /v switch shows all lines that don't contain the search string.
- The /c switch reports how many lines contain the search string.
- The /n switch gives the numbers of the lines containing the search string.
- The /i switch finds all instances of the search string, no matter what their case. (By default, the **find** command is case-sensitive; that is, it finds the exact sequence of uppercase and lowercase letters you specify.)

How to Use

To display all the lines that contain the word *affect* in the IMPACT.DOC file, enter

find "affect" impact.doc

for

for *%variable* **in** (*set*) **do** *command* [command-parameters]
for *%%variable* **in** (*set*) **do** *command* [*command-parameters*]

When to Use

You have a directory with 50 files in it. Each file is a letter to a client. You need to correct a mistake in the letter to Mr. Rutger, but you can't tell from the filename which file is his.

Use the **for** command to run the same command on a set of files. You use the first syntax on the command line and the second in batch files. See page 88 for more information on how to use the **for** command in batch files.

How to Use

Find the file containing the name "Rutger" by using **for** in conjunction with **find** on the command line, like this:

for %p in (*.*) do find /c "Rutger" %p >> found.txt

The /c switch reports the number of occurrences of the search string, and the double right angle brackets (>>) redirect the output to a file called FOUND.TXT. See page 82 for information on redirection.

format

format *drive*:[/q] [/u] [/f:*size*]
See the documentation for information about other switches.

Improved in DOS 5

When to Use

You want to format a 5.25-inch, 360 KB disk that you can use with both your office computer, which has a high-density drive, and your home computer, which has a low-density drive.

The **format** command divides the disk into small sections called *sectors*. It also creates a root directory and a file allocation table (FAT), which is a record of the locations of all the files on the disk. All disks must be formatted before DOS can use them. For more information on the **format** command see page 57.

How to Use

To format a 5.25-inch, 360 KB disk in a high-density drive by entering

format a: /f:360

goto

goto *label*

Use the **goto** command in batch files to jump to a line that you have marked with a label. See page 91 for more information about how to use this command.

graftabl

graftabl [*xxx*]

Use the **graftabl** command to enable printing of the extended characters of the indicated code page. If you don't need to display characters from a language other than English, you don't need to worry about this command. See the documentation for more information.

graphics

graphics [*type*] [[*drive*:][*path*]*filename*] [/r] [/b] [/lcd]
    [/printbox:std | /printbox:lcd]

Use the **graphics** command to enable the printing of screens generated in graphic mode or on a color monitor. See the documentation for a list of printer names.

*New
in DOS 5*

help

help [*command*]

Use the **help** command to get online information about DOS commands. Simply type *help* and the command you want to know more about, like this:

help format

A slightly quicker method to get help is to use the /? switch with any command you need help with, like this:

format /?

if

if [not] **exist** *filename command*
if [not] ***string1***==*string2 command*
if [not] **errorlevel** *number command*

Use the **if** command to have a batch file carry out different actions depending on the situation at hand. See page 90 for more information.

join

join [*drive1*: [*drive2*:]*path*]
join *drive*: /d

Use the **join** command to treat a drive as a directory.

keyb

keyb [*xx*[,[*yyy*][,[*drive*:][*path*]*filename*]]] [/e] [/id:*nnn*]

Use the **keyb** command, either on the command line or from your AUTOEXEC.BAT file, to configure your keyboard for a language other than U.S. English. See the documentation for more information.

label

label [*drive*:][*label*]

When to Use
You have a disk that holds information you gathered at trade shows you attended last year. You want to assign a volume label to the disk to distinguish it from the information you are gathering this year.

Use the **label** command to create, modify, or delete a disk's volume label. Use the **vol** command to view the label.

How to Use
Label the disk in the A drive with the name *shows90* by entering:

   label a:shows90

New in DOS 5

loadhigh

loadhigh [*drive*:][*path*]*filename* [*parameters*]

The **loadhigh** command loads the specified program into upper memory. For more information, see the documentation.

md or mkdir

md [*drive*:]*path*
mkdir [*drive*:]*path*

Use the **md** command to create a new directory (**mkdir** is an alternative form of this command). For more information about creating directories, see page 37.

mem

mem [/p|/d|/c]

When to Use

While you are running a program that converts files from one format to another, DOS displays the message *Not enough memory*. You are baffled because you have run this same program before without any problems.

Use the **mem** command to find out how much memory your computer has and how that memory is being used. When diagnosing memory-related problems, these switches can help you narrow down the list of possible culprits.

- The /p (program) switch tells **mem** to list the programs that are currently using memory.
- The /d (debug) switch is similiar to the /p switch but also includes information of interest to programmers.
- The /c (classify) switch shows where programs are loaded in conventional and upper memory. This switch can be useful if you are trying to optimize the way memory is used on your machine. See page 101 for a brief discussion of memory optimization.

How to Use

Display the type and amount of memory available on your computer by entering

    mem

For a more detailed report on memory usage, including the location of programs in conventional and upper memory, enter

mem /c

mirror

mirror [*drive*:[...]] [/1] [/t*drive*[-*entries*] [...]]
See the documentation for information about these and other switches.

When to Use

Not long ago, you accidentally formatted your hard drive. You want to avoid the trauma of having to reconstruct valuable files in the event of future mistakes.

Use the **mirror** command to make a copy of the file allocation table (FAT) and root directory of the specified drive so that the **unformat** command can restore the drive. Mirror puts the FAT and root-directory information in a file called MIRROR.FIL. If you accidentally format or somehow corrupt your hard disk, you can use the **unformat** command to reconstruct the drive using the information stored in this file.

To be effective, you must run **mirror** frequently. You might want to add the command to your AUTOEXEC.BAT file so that DOS runs it every time you start your computer.

How to Use

Run the **mirror** command by entering

mirror c:

Tell DOS to run the mirror command every time you turn on your computer, by loading your AUTOEXEC.BAT file into the DOS Editor (see page 29), entering

mirror c:

on a line by itself, and saving the file. The command is then run the next time you boot your computer. If you want **mirror** to record information about other drives, simply add them to the command, as in

mirror c: d:

mode

See the documentation for possible syntaxes.

Use the multipurpose **mode** command to configure ports or devices, display the status of installed devices, and change your display. You can also use **mode** to control how quickly DOS repeats characters when you hold down a key. Check the documentation for specific uses of the **mode** command

more

more < [*drive*:][*path*]*filename*
command | **more**

When to Use

You want to view a long file on the screen, but the first part of the file scrolls by too fast for you to read it.

Use the **more** command to display information one screenful at a time. (From within the Shell, you can use the View File Contents command on the File menu.)

The information can be the contents of a file or the output from a command. For example, you could redirect the information from the **mode** command to the **more** command so that you can view the output a screenful at a time, by entering

mode | more

(We discuss redirection on page 82.)

How to Use

View the contents of the file TEXT.TXT one screenful at a time by entering

more < text.dat

Press any key to see the next screenful, and press Ctrl-C if you have seen enough and want to cancel the command.

nlsfunc

nlsfunc [[*drive*:][*path*]*filename*]

Use the **nlsfunc** command in support of a language other than English. See the documentation for more information.

path

path [[*drive*:]*path*[;...]]

When to Use

You type the name of a program you copied to your hard disk yesterday. The program doesn't run and DOS displays the message *Bad command or filename*.

Use the **path** command to display the current path or set a new one, either directly or in your AUTOEXEC.BAT file.

DOS searches for executable commands in the directories specified by the **path** command. For example, when you install DOS, the DOS directory is included in a **path** command in your AUTOEXEC.BAT file so that DOS can find the commands in the DOS directory. You can specify as many *drive:path* combinations as you can fit on the 127-character command line.

How to Use

If the program you are trying to run is not in the current directory, it must be in your path. Enter the **path** command by itself to display the current path, like this:

    path

For information about including a command in your AUTOEXEC.BAT file, see page 29.

pause

pause

Use the **pause** command to temporarily halt batch-file processing. DOS prompts you to press a key to continue.

print

print [[*drive*:][*path*]*filename* [...]]
See the documentation for information about available switches.

When to Use

You have used the DOS Editor to create a simple list of accounts and now you want to print the list.

Use the **print** command to print this unformatted text file.

The **print** command is a terminate-and-stay-resident (TSR) program. When you use the command, it claims a certain amount of memory for its operation, and the only way to reclaim that memory is to restart your computer. The **print** command monitors CPU activity and uses the CPU to print when it isn't otherwise occupied.

When you choose the **print** command, the file you specify is added to a list called the *print queue*. You can use wildcard characters to specify several files if you want to print more than one file at a time. You can examine or modify the print queue by using the **print** command with switches. (See the documentation for explanations of these many options.)

Note that you may not be able to use the **print** command if you are working on a network. Try using the **copy** command instead, as in

copy myfile.txt lpt1

How to Use
Print the unformatted ACCOUNTS.LST file by entering

print accounts.lst

prompt

prompt [*text*]

When to Use

You want to change the default command prompt so that it greets you subserviently and gives you a feeling of being in control.

Use the **prompt** command to change your system prompt. You can add **prompt** to your AUTOEXEC.BAT file so that the prompt is always the way you want it. The *text* parameter can be any group of characters (called a *text string*) or a combination of special display codes. These codes represent text and various system variables; they consist of a dollar sign followed by a single character. The most commonly used codes are $p, which adds the current drive and path to the prompt, and $g, which adds a greater-than sign (>). If you install DOS 5 on a new or newly formatted hard drive that has no AUTOEXEC.BAT file, the installation program creates the file and includes in it a **prompt $p $g** statement.

How to Use

Change the command prompt by loading AUTOEXEC.BAT into the DOS Editor (see page 29), entering

prompt How may I help you?

on a line by itself, and saving the file. You see the new prompt the next time you boot your computer.

At any time, you can restore the default prompt (the current drive letter followed by a right angle bracket) by entering

prompt

qbasic

qbasic [[/run] [*drive*:][*path*]*filename*]
See the documentation for other switch information.

New
in DOS 5

Use the **qbasic** command to start the QBasic interpreter. The interpreter reads and carries out the Basic instructions contained in Basic programs, several of which are included in the DOS 5 package.

Note that you cannot use the DOS Editor if QBasic is not in the current directory or a directory in the **path** command.

rd or rmdir

rd [*drive*:]*path*
rmdir [*drive*:]*path*

Use the **rd** (Remove Directory) command to delete a directory (**rmdir** is an alternative form). The directory must be empty, and you must not be in the directory you want to remove. From the Shell, you can simply select the directory and press the Del key to remove it. See page 55 for more information.

recover

recover [*drive*:][*path*]*filename*

The **recover** command is an advanced command that is used to extract information from a defective disk. See the documentation for more information.

rem

rem [*comment*]

Use the **rem** command to embed messages and comments in a batch file or your CONFIG.SYS file. DOS skips over any lines that start with **rem**.

ren or rename

ren [*drive:*][*path*]*filename1 filename2*
rename [*drive:*][*path*]*filename1 filename2*

When to Use

You worked on a set of files with RPT extensions on your computer at home, and you want to copy the new versions from disk to your office computer without overwriting the old versions.

Use the **ren** (Rename) command to change the names of files stored on your office computer before copying the new versions from disk. (You can use **rename** as an alternative form of this command.)

You can use wildcard characters with the **ren** command. You cannot use this command to rename directories or rename across drives. For example,

   ren d:\accts*.doc c:\back*.bak

does not work because two drives are involved.

See page 51 for more information about this command.

How to Use
Change the extensions of the old versions of the files to BAK by entering

   ren *.rpt *.bak

replace

replace [*drive1:*][*path1*]*filename* [*drive2:*][*path2*] [/a] [/p] [/r] [/w]
replace [*drive1:*][*path1*]*filename* [*drive2:*][*path2*] [/p] [/r] [/s] [/w] [/u]

When to Use

You have several versions of a file called INVNTORY.TXT in different directories, and you have just received a new version of the file. You want to replace all the older versions with the new version.

Use the **replace** command to be sure that all the files are updated to the current version.

You can use **replace** with the following switches:

- The /a switch adds from the source directory only those files that are not already in the destination directory.
- The /p switch prompts you to confirm that you want to replace the file.
- The /r switch replaces read-only files.
- The /s switch searches subdirectories.
- The /u switch replaces only the files in the destination directory that are older than those in the source directory.
- The /w switch waits for a disk to be inserted before beginning its search for source files.

How to Use

Search the entire C drive (including subdirectories) and replace all instances of INVNTORY.TXT with the file of the same name that is on the disk in your A drive, by entering

replace a:\invntory.txt c:\ /s

restore

restore *drive1*: *drive2*:[*path*[*filename*]]
See the documentation for switch information.

When to Use

You backed up all the files in your C:\WORD\LETTERS directory to a floppy disk using the backup command. Now you want to retrieve only the files with LET extensions.

Use the **restore** command to retrieve files stored with the **backup** command. The **restore** command can be a bit confusing. It helps to remember that the backup files can be restored only to the directory from which they were backed up. You can't change the restoration path. You can, however, specify that only certain files be restored. See pages 61 and 62 for more information about backing up and restoring files.

How to Use

Retrieve only the files with LET extensions by entering

restore a: c:\word\letters*.let

The first parameter tells DOS where to find the files, and the second parameter specifies which files to restore.

set

set [*variable=[string]*]

Use the **set** command to modify DOS environment variables. New DOS users probably won't have occasion to use this command. See the documentation if you need information.

*New
in DOS 5*

setver

setver [*drive:path*][*filename n.nn*]
See the documentation for information about other switches.

Use the **setver** command to tell DOS to send a version number other than 5 to a specific program. See page 73 for more information.

share

share [*/f:space*] [*/l:locks*]

Use the **share** command in a network or multitasking environment to support file-sharing and file-locking.

shift

shift

Use the **shift** command in batch files to change the value of parameters. See the documentation for more information.

sort

sort [/r] [/+n] [<] [*drive1:*] [*path1*]*filename1*
    [>[*drive2:[path2][filename2]*]
[*command* |] **sort** [/r] [/+n] [>[*drive2:[path2][filename2]*]

When to Use

You want to sort into alphabetical order a file containing a list of your accounts.

Use the **sort** command to sort files of up to 64 KB and either display the results on the screen or redirect them to a file.

The **sort** command acts as a filter (see page 85 for more information). You can use the /r switch to sort in descending order (ascending is the default), or the /+*n* switch to sort on a specified column. The **sort** command is not case-sensitive.

How to Use

Sort the ACCOUNTS.TXT file into ascending alphabetical order by entering

sort < c:accounts.txt | more

DOS redirects the contents of ACCOUNTS.TXT to the **sort** command, which sorts the file line by line. The output of the sort is in turn redirected to the **more** command, which displays the sorted file a screenful at a time. (See page 82 for more information about redirection.)

subst

subst [*drive1*:[*drive2*:]*path*]
subst *drive1*: /d

When to Use

You need to add the C:\ACCOUNTS\PAY\CALC directory to the path command in your AUTOEXEC.BAT file, but the command is already 120 characters long (127 is the maximum length).

Use the **subst** command to assign a drive letter as a substitute for a directory name.

How to Use

Assign a drive letter to the C:\ACCOUNTS\PAY\CALC directory name by entering

subst x: c:\accounts\pay\calc

Then add the drive letter X to the **path** command in your AUTOEXEC.BAT (see page 29).

Break the association between drive X and the directory name by using the command with the /d switch. Enter

subst x: /d

sys

sys [*drive1*:][*path*] *drive2*:

Use the **sys** command to create a bootable disk by copying the hidden system files (IO.SYS and MSDOS.SYS) and the command processor (COMMAND.COM) from drive C to the disk in your floppy drive. See page 75 for more information.

time

time [*hours*:[*minutes*[:*seconds*[.*hundredths*]]]] [a|p]

When to Use

You have an older computer that does not store the data and time. When working on a project with a colleague, you forget to set the date and time on your computer. Later, you cannot tell who has the latest version of the project files.

You want to ensure that you do not forget to enter the time when you turn on your computer.

Use the **time** command to display the current time, as recorded by your computer's clock, and to change the time, if necessary. Use the a or p switch when entering times based on a 12-hour clock;for example, 4:25p is equivalent to 16:25.

If you have an older IBM PC, XT, or compatible, your computer may not store the date and time automatically. In that case, you will need to set the date and time each time you turn on the computer so that the application programs you use can assign accurate creation and modification times to the files you work with. Adding the **time** command to your AUTOEXEC.BAT file prompts you to enter the current time before doing any work.

How to Use

Change the time to 4:25 p.m. by entering

  time 16:25

Tell DOS to prompt you to enter the time, by loading your AUTOEXEC.BAT file into the DOS Editor (see page 29), entering

  time

on a line by itself, and saving the file. The next time you boot your computer, DOS displays the time that is stored by your computer's clock and prompts you to enter a new time. If you don't want to change the displayed time, simply press Enter.

tree

tree [*drive*:][*path*] [/f] [/a]

When to Use

You need a printout of your directory hierarchy.

Use the **tree** command to graphically represent the directory hierarchy of a disk or drive. The display is the same as that in the Directory Tree area of the Shell.

How to Use

Display all the subdirectories of the root directory of the current drive by entering

**tree **

Redirect the output of the **tree** command to a file by entering

tree \ > treefile.txt

To see the directory tree on paper, simply print the file.

type

type [*drive*:] [*path*]*filename*

When to Use

You want to read the installation instructions contained in the file *read.me* on the floppy disk of the new software you just purchased.

If the file is short, use the **type** command to display the contents of the file on the screen. If the file is longer than one screen, use the **more** command instead. (See page 82 for information about the **more** command.) The Shell equivalent of both of these commands is View File Contents on the File menu.

How to Use

View the read.me file on drive A by entering

type a:\read.me

New
in DOS 5

undelete

undelete [[*drive*:][*path*]*filename*] [/list | /all] [dos | /dt]

When to Use

You acccidentally entered *del *.doc* when you intended to enter *del *.bak*.

Use the **undelete** command to restore accidentally deleted files to a hard or floppy disk. The **undelete** command attempts to restore files that have been deleted with the **del** command. For the best chance of success, use **undelete** as soon as you realize you have deleted the wrong files. Any action that alters the files on the disk will make it harder to undelete files.

How to Use

Restore deleted files by moving to the directory that contained the files and entering

> **undelete**

For each file that can be recovered, you are asked whether you want to undelete the file. If you answer *yes*, you are prompted for the first letter of the filename. See page 68 for a discussion of the **undelete** command.

New
in DOS 5

unformat

unformat *drive*: [/j]
unformat *drive*: [/u] [/l] [/test] [/p]
unformat *drive*: [/partn] [/l]

When to Use

You have accidentally reformatted a floppy disk containing valuable information.

Use the **unformat** command to attempt to restore the disk. See the documentation for information about the different forms of this command.

If the disk was formatted using DOS 5, your chances of recovering its contents are good. DOS 5 saves critical information about the disk before formatting it. Earlier versions do not save the information the **unformat** command needs to restore the disk, and the results are likely to be disappointing. (See page 70 for more information.)

How to Use
Restore the contents of an accidentally formatted floppy disk in drive A by entering

unformat a:

ver

ver

Use the **ver** (Version) command on a line by itself to display the version of DOS that is running on your system. This command can be a handy troubleshooting tool, because many application programs behave differently depending on which version of DOS they are running under.

verify

verify [on|off]

When to Use
You work with critical data, and all write-to-disk operations must be performed correctly.

Use the **verify** command to tell DOS to verify that no data is written to bad sectors on the disk. See page 59 for information about bad sectors.

How to Use
To ensure the integrity of all write operations, enter

verify on

on a line by itself in your AUTOEXEC.BAT file. Note: Your system will then run slower.

For verification of individual write operations, use the /v switch with the **copy** or **xcopy** commands (see pages 51 and 61 for more information).

vol

vol [*drive*:]

Use the **vol** command to display a disk's volume label and serial number (if any). See pages 35 and 37 for information about how to create volume labels.

xcopy

xcopy *source* [*destination*] [/a | /m] [/d:*date*] [/p] [/s [/e]] [/v] [/w]
See the documentation for switch information.

When to Use

You have just purchased a new computer, and you want to set it up with a directory hierarchy that is identical to that of your old computer.

Use the **xcopy** command as a powerful variation of the **copy** command. You can copy the contents of an entire drive, including directories and subdirectories, to another drive with one **xcopy** command. Commonly used switches are:

- The /p switch makes **xcopy** prompt before overwriting a file.
- The /s switch tells **xcopy** to copy subdirectories unless they are empty.

Like the **copy** command, **xcopy** does not, by default, tell you if it is overwriting a file. Because **xcopy** can copy entire directory hierarchies, the potential for inadvertently over-writing files is great. Exercise caution or use the /p switch to verify each file as it is copied. See page 61 for additional information on **xcopy**.

How to Use

After connecting your portable computer to your office computer and designating drive C of the portable as drive Y, copy the entire contents of your office computer's drive C to the portable by entering

    xcopy c: y: /s /e

```
┌─────────────────────────────────────────────┐
│  ┌───────────────────────────────────────┐  │
│  │                                       │  │
│  │            Appendix A                 │  │
│  │                                       │  │
│  │    Notes About Installation           │  │
│  │                                       │  │
│  └───────────────────────────────────────┘  │
└─────────────────────────────────────────────┘
```

Installation of DOS 5 is handled in large part by the Setup program that comes with the package. You'll need to respond to several questions during the installation process. If you are upgrading from a previous version of DOS, you'll need to have some floppy disks handy (for storing information about your current system configuration and backing up your hard drive).

Here is a general description of the installation process, so you'll know what to expect:

1. Insert Disk 1 in drive A, and start the Setup program by typing *a:setup* from the command prompt. The Setup program displays a message telling you that it is checking your system configuration.

2. In response to the next message, label one or two disks *Uninstall1* and *Uninstall2*. You will use these disks in the unlikely event that you want to return to your previous version of DOS.

3. Setup asks whether you are working on a network and, if you are, instructs you to read Chapter 3 of the *Getting Started* booklet in the documentation package. No shortcuts here. If you use a network, you need to read this material.

4. Setup then asks if you want to back up your hard drive. If you backed up your hard drive recently, you can skip this step. If you are concerned about only a few files

on your hard drive, it might be quicker to exit the Setup program (by pressing F3) and copy those files to a floppy disk. Then restart Setup and answer *no* to the question about backing up your hard drive. If you need to back up the entire hard drive, answer *yes*. Setup then prompts you for the number of drives on your system so that it can calculate the number of floppy disks you will need to hold the information on your hard drive. If you need more disks than you have on hand, press Esc to stop the backup procedure, and then press F3 to leave the Setup program. Scrounge around for the required number of disks, and then restart the Setup program.

5. When your hard drive is backed up, or if you skip the backup step, Setup displays the information it has about your system configuration—something like this:

DOS Type   **:MS-DOS**
DOS Path   **:C:\DOS**
MS-DOS Shell **:Don't run MS-DOS Shell on startup**
Display Type   **:VGA**

Setup is almost certainly correct about the first and fourth items, DOS Type and Display Type, and you shouldn't have to change them. The second item, DOS Path, indicates where Setup will copy the DOS command programs. Use the default path, C:\DOS, unless you have good reason to change it. The third item, MS-DOS Shell, specifies whether the Shell will appear when you start your computer. You may want to skim Chapter 2 of this book for help deciding whether you want to work in the Shell or on the command line. In any event, this decision is not irrevocable—you can change your mind later.

To change any of the information in this display, press the Arrow keys to select the item you want to change, and then press Enter for a list of alternatives.

6. When Setup has the correct information, it copies files to your hard drive, prompting you for the necessary disks. When Setup finishes the installation process, it prompts you to remove the disk in drive A and then reboots the system.

That's it. DOS 5 is installed on your system. If you have any problems with installation, refer to the troubleshooting chapter of the *Getting Started* booklet. If you need to go back to your old version of DOS, see page 74.

Index

Symbols and Numbers

Acknowledgments

Many, many thanks to Jabe Blumenthal.

About Online Press

Founded in 1986, Online Press is a group of publishing professionals working to make the presentation and access of information manageable, efficient, accurate, and economical. In 1991 we began publishing our popular *Quick Course* computer-book series, offering streamlined instruction for today's busy professional. At Online Press, it is our goal to help computer users quickly learn what they need to know about today's most popular software programs to get their work done efficiently.

Cover design and photography by Tom Draper Design
Interior text design by Salley Oberlin, Joyce Cox, and Kjell Swedin
Graphics by Pat Kervran
Layout by Joyce Cox and Polly Urban
Printed by Viking Press Inc.
Otabind® cover by Muscle Bound Bindery

Text composition by Online Press in Times Roman, with display type in Helvetica Narrow Bold, using Ventura Publisher and the Linotronic 300 laser imagesetter.

Other *Quick Course*™ Books

Don't miss the other titles in our *Quick Course*™ series! Quality books at the unbeatable price of $12.95.

AVAILABLE NOW!

- *A Quick Course*™ *in Windows*™
- *A Quick Course*™ *in WordPerfect*®
- *A Quick Course*™ *in DOS*

COMING SOON!

- *A Quick Course*™ *in Excel for Windows*™
- *A Quick Course*™ *in Word for Windows*™
- *A Quick Course*™ *in Lotus 1-2-3*®

And more...